new start for single moms

participant's guide

about the author

An effective speaker, writer, and teacher, **Diane Strack** has been involved in various aspects of women's ministry for thirty years. She is the founder and author of *New Start for Single Moms*, a highly successful mentoring and Bible study program. With her husband of thirty-five years, Dr. Jay Strack, she co-founded Student Leadership University, a global, comprehensive leadership training program for students. Diane is the coauthor of *Good Kids Who Do Bad Things* and the *Experience Scripture* study guides, including *Worship in the Storm*. She is also the contributing editor of the *IMPACT Student Bible*. Utilizing her background as an author, teacher, and life management facilitator, Diane has the ability to present both the practical and inspirational in a unique way that impacts lives. She is the proud mom of two daughters, Missy and Christina, who both serve in ministry, mother-in-law of Reverend Brent Crowe, and grandmother to Charis Rose and Gabriel Joseph Crowe.

special thanks

Heartfelt love and thanks to the many friends and staff of First Baptist Orlando who joined me in the call to minister to single-parent families, and whose dedication in time and love has made *New Start for Single Moms* a success.

Special gratitude to Dr. David Ferguson who gave me an understanding of relational Christianity in its purest form.

Thank you to my husband of thirty-five years, Jay, and my daughters, Missy and Chris, my greatest encouragers and the joys of my life.

new start for single moms

participant's guide

DIANE STRACK

THOMAS NELSON
Since 1798

NASHVILLE   DALLAS   MEXICO CITY   RIO DE JANEIRO   BEIJING

Published in Nashville, Tennessee, by Thomas Nelson. Thomas Nelson is a trademark of Thomas Nelson, Inc.

Thomas Nelson, Inc. titles may be purchased in bulk for educational, business, fund-raising, or sales promotional use. For information, please e-mail SpecialMarkets@ThomasNelson.com.

Scripture quotations, unless otherwise noted, are taken from THE NEW KING JAMES VERSION. Copyright © 1982 by Thomas Nelson, Inc. Used by permission. All rights reserved.

Scripture quotations marked NCV are taken from the New Century Version®. Copyright © 2005 by Thomas Nelson, Inc. Used by permission. All rights reserved.

Scripture quotations marked NIV are taken from the HOLY BIBLE: NEW INTERNATIONAL VERSION®. Copyright © 1973, 1978, 1984 by International Bible Society. Used by permission of Zondervan Publishing House. All rights reserved.

Scripture quotations marked NLT are taken from the *Holy Bible*, New Living Translation. Copyright © 1996, 2004 by Tyndale Charitable Trust. Used by permission of Tyndale House Publishers, Inc., Wheaton, Illinois 60189. All rights reserved.

Scripture quotations marked MSG are taken from *The Message* by Eugene H. Peterson. Copyright © 1993, 1994, 1995, 1996, 2000, 2001, 2002. Used by permission of NavPress Publishing Group. All rights reserved.

New Start for Single Moms Participant's Guide
ISBN: 978-1-4185-2801-0

Printed in the United States of America.
07 08 09 10 11 VIC 9 8 7 6 5 4 3 2 1

contents

one

let go of the past: take hold of the future

> The LORD says, "Forget what happened before, and do not think about the past. Look at the new thing I am going to do. It is already happening. Don't you see it? I will make a road in the desert and rivers in the dry land." (Isaiah 43:18–19 NCV)

The story of Abraham, Sarah (or Sarai), and Hagar is the story of victims, villains, and volunteers. It is much like your story or the stories of others you know. The good news is that a life of victory is available to everyone and anyone!

> Sarai, Abram's wife, had no children . . . [she] said to Abram, "Look, the LORD has not allowed me to have children, so have sexual relations with my slave girl." . . . Abram did what Sarai said . . . and she (Hagar) became pregnant. . . . Then Sarai said to Abram, "This is your fault." . . . Then Sarai was hard on Hagar, and Hagar ran away. (Genesis 16:1–6 NCV)

It sounded like a good idea at the time. Sarah thought she needed to help God keep His promise, so she came up with a plan. Do you ever feel God isn't paying attention and take matters in your own hands? Although you may mean well, trouble usually follows.

Look at God's promise to Abraham in Genesis chapter 15: "You will have a son." This was not a "maybe"; it was a sure promise. One thing you must believe as you start a new journey with God is that He does what He says He will do, but He has a certain timing for the events of your life just as He did in Sarah's life.

There is no doubt that Hagar was a victim in this situation. To cope with the stress, she ran away to the wilderness—probably to hide, possibly to think, maybe to try and punish Abraham and Sarah. For whatever reason, she found herself alone in the wilderness.

Have you ever felt that you were in the wilderness of aloneness? It is a horrible feeling, isn't it? No direction for life and the feeling that no one cares.

Did God have a plan for Hagar? Yes, He did. Does He have a plan for you? Yes, He does! Genuine, growing relationships with God and other persons are the sole cure for aloneness. Other behaviors might mask aloneness, but only God's plan can heal it. A genuine relationship is God's idea. He created the desire within us because He longs to be intimate with us, His creation. It can and should be experienced in every dimension of our being—spirit, soul, and body—in a continual way, never dependent on feeling or circumstances. Don't be willing to settle for imposters such as sexual or emotional intimacy or conditional bonding.

the meaning of a genuine relationship

YAD (Hebrew)—*to know deeply.* This word is used in Psalm 139:1–4 to express God's deep personal awareness and understanding of us. He knew us from our mother's womb and is acquainted with our every thought, emotion, and motivation. And the good news is that His love is unconditional, meaning that He loves us deeply even though He knows our innermost thoughts.

> O LORD, You have searched me and known me. You know my sitting down and my rising up; You understand my thought afar off. You comprehend my path and my lying down, And are acquainted with all my ways. For there is not a word on my tongue, But behold, O LORD, You know it altogether. (Psalm 139:1–4)

SAKAN (Hebrew)—*living together, to make a home together.* God wants to dwell in your heart and be the foundation for your home. This beneficial or caring involvement is the hallmark of a genuine relationship.

> And this is the reason: God lives forever and is holy. He is high and lifted up. He says, "I live in a high and holy place, but I also live with people who are sad and humble. I give new life to those who are humble and to those whose hearts are broken. (Isaiah 57:15 NCV)

Here is the message you must believe: the holy, all-powerful God is willing to help you, He is able to help you, and *He will most certainly help you!*

Many adults fear a genuine, intimate relationship because they were hurt either as children by someone who knew them well and abused or took advantage of them, or as an adult by someone with whom they were in a close relationship. God wants to heal your hurt through an understanding of His unconditional love and His deep, personal care for you.

If you feel like you are in a desert today, there is good news! God is making provision to give you great joy, an abundant life.

> The angel of the LORD found Hagar beside a desert spring along the road to Shur. The angel said to her, "Hagar, Sarai's servant, where have you come from, and where are you going?"
>
> "I am running away from my mistress," she replied. (Genesis 16:7–8 NLT)

What a beautiful picture of our proactive God! Our precious Lord knew Hagar was in such despair she could not come to Him, so He went to her. Notice that God asked Hagar, "Where have you come from, and where are you going?" (v. 8). Why ask if He already knew? The same reason He asks you now where you are going: we must always stop to think about where our reactions will take us and what we will accomplish through our choices.

God is asking you, "Where have you come from and where are you going?" Wherever you are at this moment, He is ready to meet you there, just as you are—but He loves you too much to leave you there.

> And the angel also said, "You are now pregnant and will give birth to a son. You are to name him Ishmael (which means 'God hears'), for the LORD has heard about your misery." (Genesis 16:11 NLT)

Hagar sat in pain, feeling as though no one cared, when suddenly the announcement was made: "You are to name him Ishmael, (which means 'God hears')" (v. 11). How those two words must have given her joy and strength. God hears! Every time she called the name of *Ishmael*, she remembered, *God hears my thoughts.* Understanding God's personal love and care for your life is a powerful healer and gives confidence for the future. In fact, with that short conversation, Hagar was able to go home and resume her life.

But then fourteen years passed by and Hagar, a single mom, began to be hated by her mistress.

Sarah became pregnant and gave birth to a son. (Genesis 21:2 NCV)

Isaac grew . . . But Sarah saw Ishmael making fun of Isaac . . . So Sarah said to Abraham, "Throw out this slave woman and her son." . . . Early the next morning Abraham took some food and a leather bag full of water. He gave them to Hagar and sent her away . . . Hagar went and wandered in the desert. (Genesis 21:8–10, 14 NCV)

Once again Abraham listened to Sarah's reactive personality and sent Hagar out to the wilderness, hoping to end the problem by throwing it out. She was abandoned, literally tossed out into the desert. Her child support payment was some food and a skin of water. Not much to start with, even less to raise a child on, and her bitterness and despair continued to grow.

When the water was gone, she left the boy in the shade of a bush. Then she went and sat down by herself about a hundred yards away. "I don't want to watch the boy die," she said, as she burst into tears. (Genesis 21:15–16 NLT)

This time Hagar didn't just visit the wilderness of despair, she moved in. Notice that *she sat down*; in other words, she gave up. Depression overwhelmed her, and Hagar turned her back on the child as she wept uncontrollably. She lost all hope when she allowed the barren wilderness around her to move into her mind and heart. Many of us can relate to this feeling. Let's see what God did for Hagar and what He will do for you.

the God who hears

God heard the boy crying, and God's angel called to Hagar from heaven. He said, "What is wrong, Hagar? Don't be afraid! God has heard the boy crying there.". . . Then God showed Hagar a well of water. So she went to the well and filled her bag with water and gave the boy a drink. God was with the boy as he grew up. (Genesis 21:17–21 NCV)

Again the Lord asked questions because He wanted Hagar to think through the future. He knows our fears, our loneliness, our despair. But, He asks, "Do you know about Me? Do you know My love and provision?"

Verse 19 is the KEY. God opened her eyes and she saw the well of water! If you will allow Him to open your eyes to His provision for you, you will also see the flow of blessings that the Lord longs to give.

Man gave her a bottle of water. God gave her a well!

He wants to do the same for you by giving you a new view of life! No longer should you focus on the wilderness and the empty bottle. Instead, He wants to show you a well of peace, joy, and life that will never run dry. Listen as He calls to you from heaven, as He speaks to you through His Word:

> The LORD says, "Forget about what happened before, and do not think about the past. Look at the new thing I am going to do. It is already happening. Don't you see it? I will make a road in the desert and rivers in the dry land." (Isaiah 43:18–19 NCV)

The Lord promises to provide for our needs and to give us an abundance of life. We must be willing to trust Him because He cares for us and sees our future as clearly as we can see yesterday.

> And my God shall supply all your need according to His riches in glory by Christ Jesus. (Philippians 4:19)

Understand the scope of that verse: ALL of your needs—motional, spiritual, relational, and physical. All of this is met through the riches available in Christ Jesus.

Abraham sent her away; God came looking for her.

Man gave her a bottle of water; God gave her a well.

Hagar's extreme need became God's great opportunity. Your need is God's great opportunity. He longs to do a new thing for you. See, He has already begun!

We have talked about where you are coming from; now let us focus on where you are going.

"Being proactive means more than taking initiative.
It means that we take responsibility for our lives.
Instead of blaming circumstances, conditions,
or chance for our behavior, we choose our
own responses and make our own decisions."
—STEPHEN COVEY

circle two or three LIFE AREAS that you would like to begin a change in:

SPIRITUAL:
Intimacy with God, prayer life, studying the Bible

FAMILY:
Relationships with siblings, parents, children, father of your children

PERSONAL DEVELOPMENT:
Skills, hobbies, sports, seminars, classes

LEISURE TIME/SOCIAL:
Friendships, clubs, groups, activities

PROFESSIONAL:
Career development, education

CHURCH/COMMUNITY:
Leadership in activities and events, volunteering

HEALTH:
Nutrition, exercise, weight management

HOUSEHOLD:
Organizing, cleaning, decorating

FINANCIAL:
Financial freedom, saving, investing, budgeting

The Dream Worksheet is the tool that will allow you to break your goals down into achievable steps and empower you to make your dreams come true! Use the worksheets on the following pages and follow the Sample Dream Worksheet as a guideline.

SAMPLE dream worksheet

"A goal is a dream
with detailed direction
and a deadline."
—JAY STRACK

WHY DO I WANT TO DO THIS? Select one of the Life Areas and write two or three sentences that describe what you want to change about this area of your life.

FINANCIAL SECURITY: Because God's part is to be faithful to provide and my part is to be faithful with what He provides, preparing for the future for my children, and able to live without worry or fear.

WHAT DO I WANT TO DO? Get very specific about the goal and describe it in a few sentences for your own understanding.

To successfully live within my financial means; to provide for my children; to be prepared for financial emergencies such as repairs and medical bills; to live peaceably without fear of a budget crisis.

WHEN SHOULD THE OVERALL GOAL BE COMPLETED? A goal must have detailed direction and a deadline to remove it from the pile of *somedays.* Assign a realistic date and write it down to keep yourself accountable.

Twelve weeks from today

HOW I PLAN TO ACHIEVE MY DREAM: By breaking down the goal into small steps, your dream becomes attainable. Write out the steps and assign an order to each one of 1, 2, 3, etc. Then assign a deadline date to each step. Note that flexibility is key. The deadline is for your own accountability, but if circumstances cause you to miss it, make a written change. Never abandon your goals or steps.

ORDER	INTERMEDIATE STEPS	DEADLINE
1.	fill out my budget sheet	this week
2.	pray in faith: Philippians 4:6–8	every week
3.	identify needs vs. wants	within the next 2 weeks
4.	faithful in giving back: Malachi 3:10	begin next paycheck
5.	continue to give my best: Matthew 25:14–30	every day
6.	make appointment with financial advisor	next week
7.	incorporate changes	in the next 4 weeks
8.	start an envelope system: Proverbs 6:6–8	week 8

dream worksheet

"A goal is a dream
with detailed direction
and a deadline."
—JAY STRACK

WHY DO I WANT TO DO THIS? Select one of the Life Areas and write two or three sentences that describe what you want to change about this area of your life.

_____

_____

_____

_____

_____

WHAT DO I WANT TO DO? Get very specific about the goal and describe it in a few sentences for your own understanding.

_____

_____

_____

_____

_____

WHEN SHOULD THE OVERALL GOAL BE COMPLETED? A goal must have detailed direction and a deadline to remove it from the pile of *somedays.* Assign a realistic date and write it down to keep yourself accountable.

_____

_____

_____

_____

_____

HOW I PLAN TO ACHIEVE MY DREAM: By breaking down the goal into small steps, your dream becomes attainable. Write out the steps and assign an order to each one of 1, 2, 3, etc. Then assign a deadline date to each step. Note that flexibility is key. The deadline is for your own accountability, but if circumstances cause you to miss it, make a written change. Never abandon your goals or steps.

ORDER (1, 2, 3, etc.)	INTERMEDIATE STEPS	DEADLINE

dream worksheet

*"A goal is a dream
with detailed direction
and a deadline."*
—Jay Strack

WHY DO I WANT TO DO THIS? Select one of the Life Areas and write two or three sentences that describe what you want to change about this area of your life.

_____

_____

_____

_____

_____

WHAT DO I WANT TO DO? Get very specific about the goal and describe it in a few sentences for your own understanding.

_____

_____

_____

_____

_____

WHEN SHOULD THE OVERALL GOAL BE COMPLETED? A goal must have detailed direction and a deadline to remove it from the pile of *somedays.* Assign a realistic date and write it down to keep yourself accountable.

_____

_____

_____

_____

_____

HOW I PLAN TO ACHIEVE MY DREAM: By breaking down the goal into small steps, your dream becomes attainable. Write out the steps and assign an order to each one of 1, 2, 3, etc. Then assign a deadline date to each step. Note that flexibility is key. The deadline is for your own accountability, but if circumstances cause you to miss it, make a written change. Never abandon your goals or steps.

ORDER (1, 2, 3, etc.)	INTERMEDIATE STEPS	DEADLINE

dream worksheet

*"A goal is a dream
with detailed direction
and a deadline."*
—Jay Strack

WHY DO I WANT TO DO THIS? Select one of the Life Areas and write two or three sentences that describe what you want to change about this area of your life.

_____

_____

_____

_____

_____

WHAT DO I WANT TO DO? Get very specific about the goal and describe it in a few sentences for your own understanding.

_____

_____

_____

_____

_____

WHEN SHOULD THE OVERALL GOAL BE COMPLETED? A goal must have detailed direction and a deadline to remove it from the pile of *somedays.* Assign a realistic date and write it down to keep yourself accountable.

_____

_____

_____

_____

_____

HOW I PLAN TO ACHIEVE MY DREAM: By breaking down the goal into small steps, your dream becomes attainable. Write out the steps and assign an order to each one of 1, 2, 3, etc. Then assign a deadline date to each step. Note that flexibility is key. The deadline is for your own accountability, but if circumstances cause you to miss it, make a written change. Never abandon your goals or steps.

ORDER (1, 2, 3, etc.)	INTERMEDIATE STEPS	DEADLINE

my 10-week
commitment to *new start*

*"God-confidence reckons that we, in ourselves,
have huge limitations, but that God does not.
God-confidence is the belief that we can do
anything God gives us to do."*
—CAROL KENT & KAREN LEE-THORP

Believing that God has a wonderful plan for my life,
I pledge to complete the ten weekly sessions
through the *New Start for Single Moms* program.
I will give my best, by faith,
because God has already given His Best for me.

_____   _____

Signature of mom   Date

_____   _____

Signature of mentor   Date

The LORD says, "Forget what happened before, and do
not think about the past. Look at the new thing I am going
to do. It is already happening. Don't you see it?"
(Isaiah 43:18–19 NCV)

two

the power of
genuine relationships

A genuine relationship with God is the starting point of an emotionally healthy life, but He also created us with a desire to interact on an intimate level with people. Meeting emotional and relational needs through relationships has always been God's plan. In fact, these were a vital part of the earthly life of Christ.

During His years on earth, Jesus had three single friends who He loved dearly: Martha, Mary, and Lazarus. Their relationships were genuine, and they were not afraid to express their needs to one another.

> Martha had a sister named Mary, who was sitting at Jesus' feet and listening to him teach. But Martha was busy with all the work to be done. She went in and said, "Lord, don't you care that my sister has left me alone to do all the work? Tell her to help me." But the Lord answered her, "Martha, Martha, you are worried and upset about many things. Only one thing is important. Mary has chosen the better thing, and it will never be taken away from her." (Luke 10:38–42 NCV)

In this passage, we see Martha focused on meeting the physical needs of Jesus. This was a good choice, but she focused so heavily on it she did not see the other side of hospitality; that is, meeting the relational and emotional needs.

She **reacted** to the stress of the task with her "It's not fair" speech.

Jesus quickly **responded** with a teaching point, one that you and I must learn. Notice His reply:

> Martha, you are worried and upset about many things . . .
> Mary has chosen the better thing, and it will never be taken
> away. (vv. 41–42)

Let's relate this to our lives. We are distracted, stressed, busy with all the good and important tasks that must be done, and, as a result, we neglect the **best** thing— the meeting of emotional-relational needs for ourselves and our loved ones. This choice, Jesus pointed out, will never be taken away from us because healthy relationships will forever impact our lives and those with whom we are involved.

On a scale of difficulty, this choice should be the easiest, but is it? Can we hold still? Can we believe in the value of something we cannot visibly see the result of or physically hold in our hands?

Mary was sitting at the feet of Jesus, listening to Him teach. What value was there in Mary doing that when Jesus came into town hungry, tired, and dusty? A great deal. Martha looked into His eyes and saw the physical need; Mary looked into those same eyes and saw an emotional need—He needed someone to believe in Him! He needed a full, face-to-face time of listening, smiling, nodding encouragement, and caring for His soul. He needed to see that His life and teaching were valuable, and that they could be a blessing to this woman and others.

A powerful exchange happened in that quiet corner of the room as each friend gave and received.

REACT: It's all about ME!

RESPOND: It's about the situation and how it can be improved or resolved.

Martha reacted; Jesus responded.

Let's look at a second situation in this friendship:

> Now a certain man was sick, Lazarus of Bethany, the town of Mary and her sister Martha . . . Therefore, the sisters sent to Him saying, "Lord behold, he whom You love is sick." . . . Now Martha said to Jesus, "Lord, if You had been here, my brother would not have died.". . . Jesus said to her, "Your brother will rise again." Martha said to Him, "I know that he will rise again in the resurrection at the last day." Jesus said to her, "I am the resurrection and the life. He who believes in Me, though he may die, he will live. And whoever lives and believes in Me shall never die. Do you believe this?" She said to Him, "Yes, Lord, I believe that You are the Christ, the Son of God, who is to come into the world." (John 11:1–5, 21–27)

Once again Jesus met relational needs in this friendship. The sisters sent word asking Him to come, but as soon as He did Martha spit out, "It's your fault. If you had come earlier when we first called you, this wouldn't have happened!" Martha was awfully good at reacting and playing the blame game!

Jesus responded to Martha's reaction. He saw that her irrational emotional outburst was really a symptom of a spiritual need. He asked the question, "Do you believe?" Martha said the right words: "Yes, I believe," but she did not allow this faith to be genuine. It did not control her life or make a difference in her emotions.

Before we go any further, you must answer that question yourself: Do I really believe that Jesus holds the key to all the needs in my life?

Emotional—Relational—Physical—Spiritual

Are there spiritual voids in my life that might be disguised as emotional needs?

Read Jay Strack's story about unhealthy relationships and healing:

When I was six years old, my father walked out with another woman. Night after night, I prayed that God would send my daddy home, but it didn't happen. The message I got from my dad's abandonment was: "Jay, you're a loser. You're nobody. You're not important to me, and I don't want you in my life."

After my dad left, my mother worked two or three jobs, trying to hold together what was left of our family. My mom dated a lot of guys, and every man she was attracted to was someone she had met in a bar—in other words, a guy with an alcohol problem. She had already been abandoned by an alcoholic husband, yet she kept going back to guys who were just like him or worse. On more than one occasion, as a little boy at the time, I would get out my Louisville Slugger baseball bat and threaten the man who was beating my mom or beating me. I had a really good seat for that.

I would say, "Mom, let's get someone to help us," but she was too embarrassed. "Let's wait until the bruises heal" or "Let's see if I can get us some clothes first." She wanted to hide her pain behind furniture, clothes, and plastic smiles.

I got used to the men moving in and out of our house until the summer that one of the men brought his older son. That was the summer I learned about sexual abuse. After six or so men moved in and out, one moved in who promised to stay. He said, "Jay, you can call me Dad, and I will treat you like my own son." I was so excited to have a dad again that I went to school the next day and told all my friends about him. But before long, Bob was staying out late, drinking.

One night, Bob was out late, and my mom said, "If he doesn't leave that bar, I'm divorcing him!" But I was ten years old and I wanted a dad. I thought I could talk him into coming home and everything would be okay, so I went to the bar and found Bob sitting and drinking with his buddies. With tears I pleaded, "You promised to be my dad. Please come home."

Bob said, "Jay, I tell you what—if you'll get on your knees and beg me, I'll come home and be your dad." So I got down on my knees and begged. And what did Bob do? He started laughing at me. And all the other men in that bar started laughing along with him.

My face turned dark, but my heart became hard. The tears would no longer flow. It was as if someone had turned a light off inside me. Mom had her own pain to deal with, and I decided I would never ask anybody for anything again.

I blamed God for all the pain in my life, for the fact that my dad left us, and for my alcoholic step-dads, for the fights and violence in our home, for the adultery that kept ripping our home apart, for the abuse that scarred me. By the time I became a teenager, I stopped blaming God. Why? Because I had stopped believing in God.

What followed was a life of drugs, alcohol, and arrest records. Nothing could change the path of destruction I chose. I began as a victim, but soon I was the villain of my own life, making one poor choice after another. I'll never forget the first time I heard about a personal relationship with Jesus. One of those "Jesus Freaks" at school started telling me that he had invited Christ into his life. When he told me that God wanted to be my Father, I laughed. "Who needs a father? If God is a father like my father, forget it!" Inside I was dying, and I knew I needed help. But that night on my knees in the bar, I decided I would never ask for help again. And so I continued to be a volunteer, willingly giving up any chance at a normal life.

What everyone saw as destructive behavior, I knew was a deep emotional need for a genuine relationship with a parent and with God. God knew it too, and He came looking for me. I'll never forget the night I heard the truth of God's unconditional love for me—I thought it was too good to be true. The only thing I could manage to pray was, "God, here is my life. If you are real, show me." I was seventeen years old, and my life has never been the same.

From the first day, God began to heal me and I began to understand love, but it has taken many years for me to be able to freely give and receive unconditionally. Over thirty years later, I am enjoying not only my marriage and children, but also my grandchildren. He has allowed me to share my story and His hope with millions of people around the world. It has been a great journey, and I am confident it will continue to be so.

Whatever pain you carry from the past—abandonment, scars, embarrassment, or shame—you can give it to God today. He loves you.

Lazarus died, but Jesus called him forth from the grave to new life. He can do the same for you. When your day seems like it can't get any worse, then you know Jesus is about to do a new thing in you. God wants to give you His heart; in fact, He created us because He wanted to love us and be loved by us. He vividly demonstrated this love by offering Himself on the cross:

> This is how God showed his love to us: He sent his one and
> only Son into the world so that we could have life through

him. This is what real love is: It is not our love for God; it is
God's love for us. He sent his Son to die in our place to take
away our sins. . . . We love because God first loved us. (1
John 4:9–10, 19 NCV)

The same intense love that compelled Christ to face the cross and to forgive
His foes publicly is the same love available to us.

You **can** have healthy relationships.
You can both **give and receive** love.

Meeting emotional and relational needs through friendships has always
been God's plan. In fact, relationships were a vital part of the earthly life of
Christ. God created us to need others. Why? Think about what it would be
like if you didn't need help, love, intimacy, involvement, or interaction with
God or anyone else. His love for us is so intense, so deep, that He created us
with a need for Him in order to draw us to His love. This neediness also
forces us to look beyond ourselves for that which we need, learning to love
and trust in the process. It means that we learn the very essence of relationship as we understand that Jesus left the splendor of heaven to walk in
poverty on the earth so that He might understand firsthand our pain and
struggles. He truly wants to know us intimately and longs for a relationship
with us. Jesus showed His need for others by choosing twelve disciples as intimate confidants, traveling partners, and friends. He spent time with his single
friends, Martha, Mary, and Lazarus, on several occasions, and their friendship was clearly genuine.

Look at the basic human emotional needs on the chart that follows and choose four needs that most represent your top emotional needs. What do you think family, friends, or co-workers could do to meet these needs?

accepted	confident	in control	reassured
accepting	developed	included	recognized
accomplished	educated	independent	relaxed
acknowledged	empowered	interested	respected
admired	enouragement	knowledgeable	safe
affection	focused	listened to	satisfied
alive	forgiven	loved	secure
amused	forgiving	needed	significant
appreciated	free	noticed	successful
appreciative	fulfilled	open	supported
approved of	grown or growing	optimistic	treated fairly
attention	happy	powerful	understanding
capable	heard	privacy	understood
challenged	helped	productive	useful
clear (not confused)	helpful	protected	valued
comfort	important	proud	worthy
competent			

my top 4 emotional/relational needs

1. _____
2. _____
3. _____
4. _____

What do I do that gets in the way of others meeting my relational needs?
(For example: self-reliance, selfishness, self-condemnation, negative talk, living in the past, anger coloring my decisions and choices, etc.)

_____
_____
_____
_____
_____

How can I work toward finding people to meet these relational needs?
(For example: volunteering in the community, joining Bible study classes, single-parent groups, setting aside time to make friends, working on family relationships, etc.)

_____
_____
_____
_____
_____

How can I work on better expressing these unmet needs to the people around me who are unable or unwilling to meet them?

_____

_____

_____

_____

_____

Reacting triggers anger in both parties;
    leaves the conflict unsolved;
    creates more conflict and turmoil;
    and causes relationships to weaken or dissolve.

Can you think of an example of how a situation was unproductive by reacting?

Responding allows me to:
    communicate clearly;
    find resolution for conflict;
    accomplish my goals;
    and strengthen and maintain relationships.

How could the above situation come out differently if you responded instead?

Emotional and relational needs must be met on a continuing basis. These cannot be "stored up" even though we can survive periods of time when they are not met. Ultimately, we suffer because our needs for attention, support, appreciation, respect, and other emotional needs must be replenished repeatedly, much like our physical needs of water, sleep, and air. Another important part of our relationship with God is our devotional life. Take advantage of the Praise Worksheets that can be found on the CD-ROM or at www.newstart4moms.org. These take little time but can be powerful tools in your life as you practice thinking positively.

three
healing emotional pain—part I

Today we are going to focus on being able to freely and correctly relate to family and friends and on being able to look toward the future with God-given confidence. The goal is not just to survive disappointment but to thrive. This is possible when we allow our scarred, damaged heart to be replaced with God's healthy, loving heart. No one has ever lived without experiencing hurt. It happens—accidentally or on purpose—it happens. Even Jesus experienced pain, and we know those closest to Him were hurt.

His mother, Mary, must have looked at Him hanging in agony on the cross and remembered the angel's words, "Do not be afraid. You will become pregnant and give birth to a Son, and you will name him Jesus" (Luke 1:30–31 NCV). She knew this day of death would come—it had to. But her heart ached as the world suddenly spun out of control. The disciples felt it too. Their hopes and dreams were about to shatter. They had given up jobs, left behind family and friends, all because they believed that Jesus would change the world; and, for a while, it seemed He would. The crowds grew daily, and people loved Him. All over the land people talked of this Jesus, and they even welcomed Him to town with a parade of palms. But that was before. On this day, He told them, "In a little while you will see me no more" (John 16:16 NIV). Mary was afraid. The disciples felt abandoned, frightened, disappointed, and perhaps even angry. Jesus responded to their fears with these words:

> Don't let this throw you. You trust God, don't you? Trust me.
> (John 14:1 MSG)

Perhaps you remember a time when life was all wonderful roses—you felt love, and you gave love. Life was good. Then, through various circumstances, you found yourself alone. Jesus reminds you, "Don't let this throw you . . . trust me" (v. 1 MSG). You may be thinking, *Why should I trust him?*

First, because He loves you and wants the best for your life. That's what love is.

Second, because He understands what it feels like to be abandoned, betrayed, misunderstood, used, and abused. He speaks to you not as one who has never felt pain, but as one who has experienced personal, deep betrayal. Look at some of the people who let Jesus down in His life on earth:

INTIMATE FRIEND: Judas, one of his trusted disciples and dear friends, used a kiss to betray Him. "Immediately [Judas] went up to Jesus and said, 'Greetings Rabbi!' and kissed Him. . . . Then they came and laid hands on Jesus and took Him" (Matthew 26:48–50). Judas betrayed a trusted friendship for a handful of money.

PARTNER IN MINISTRY: Peter, His right-hand man. Jesus loved Peter and trusted him as one of His closest friends and partners in ministry. But Jesus knew what was in the heart of Peter and He said,

"Assuredly, I say to you that this night, before the rooster crows, you will deny Me three times" (Matthew 26:34). And Peter did just that. Instead of standing with Jesus in trouble, Peter folded and betrayed His friend.

FAMILY, THE CIRCLE OF FRIENDS, AND FOLLOWERS: Day after day, Jesus traveled and spoke. He was tired, hungry, and often lonely. I am sure that many times He looked for His family to stand with Him, but, alas, many of them also deserted Him. Scripture tells us that "when His own people heard about this (His teaching), they went out to lay hold of Him, for they said, 'He is out of His mind'" (Mark 3:21). Jesus was misunderstood and abandoned by those closest to Him.

RELIGIOUS LEADERS: Surely the Jewish priests and scribes would understand—surely they would read the prophecies about Him and support Him—but they did not. In fact, we read that "He did not want to walk in Judea, because the Jews sought to kill Him" (John 7:1).

Jesus understands your pain right now. He knows how you feel. He understood the pain and fear that the disciples felt as He prepared to face the cross. But He had good news for them, and today He has good news for you. What seemed like the worst possible scenario—Jesus beaten, bleeding, abandoned to die on a cross—was the beginning of the most powerful story in history; that is, the resurrection. Jesus has indeed risen from the dead, victorious over sin and death. Today He offers that same victory to you for your emotions, your mind, and your spirit.

Remember, the **SAME LOVE** that allowed Jesus to suffer pain and go to the cross for you and me is the **SAME LOVE** that empowers you to forgive and move forward. And the **SAME POWER** that broke the chains of death is the

SAME POWER that empowers you to live as a **Victor** in life over any circumstance. Believe it!

SAME LOVE, SAME POWER!!!

How do we get started? With a

FRAMEWORK FOR HEALING:
Focus on the Facts
Face My Feelings
Feed My Faith
Forgive My Foes

focus on the facts

Fact One: Thought patterns have to be corrected before we can begin to heal and move forward. Let's look at some of the distorted thinking that we allow to color our feelings, and at what we should think instead so we don't become a **Victim**.

DON'T THINK: *The offender is a horrible, worthless villain.*

Even as you hear that sentence, you have that offender in your mind. And you think, yes, he or she is horrible. This may be the hardest choice you ever make, but it is the beginning of healing. Allow yourself to understand him or her and the offense so that you can separate yourself from it.

THINK INSTEAD: *He or she is also a Victim of others' offenses.* The offender has a "worth" that is separate from his or her transgression (sin). God loves every person and died to save every person. He hates our sin but loves us.

DON'T THINK: *He or she had no excuse to treat me like that.*

THINK INSTEAD: *Sin is inexcusable, but understandable.* We must remember that all of us are sinners and capable of anything. Romans 3:23 tells us that it is the nature of man to make good and bad choices.

The first two thought patterns have to do with the offender, but these next two can change you from a **Victim** to a **Victor. Victors** focus on who God is, and not on themselves. We know that no matter what our personal experience of defeat or failure may be, Jesus is never defeated. When it seemed His death was the end of all hope for His followers, He showed them victory over death and sin. His resurrection teaches us about eternity, yes; but we also learn from Him that the death of our dreams will be followed by a resurrection of hope in God's great love for us and His personal plans for our lives. We can dream again, love again, and rejoice in Him.

DON'T THINK: *My personal worth is determined by the offender's choices and words concerning me.*

THINK INSTEAD: *I am created in the image of a loving, awesome God; created by His heart and fashioned by His hand.* I do not have to be approved by my offender because I am loved and accepted by God. I was created by God, in His image, for a personal relationship. Wow, He made me to be like Him! (See Genesis 1:26)

DON'T THINK: *I never want to risk loving anyone again because it hurts too much.*

THINK INSTEAD: *I can and will love again because God's love is too great to keep to myself. The joy of His love can and will overcome my personal pain.* (See Jeremiah 31:3)

Fact Two: God is on my side! "For I know the thoughts that I think toward you, says the Lord, thoughts of peace and not of evil, to give you a future and a hope. Then you will call upon Me and go and pray to Me, and I will listen to you" (Jeremiah 29:11–12).

- **You** are on the mind and heart of God.
  He wants to give **you** a FUTURE, literally, "an expected end."
  A HOPE, literally, "a sure thing."

- He is listening to **your** needs. He longs to hear from **you** in prayer, and He wants to bless **you.** Can you even imagine such a wonderful thing?

ME + GOD = A Majority!

"I know I am somebody
'cause God don't make no junk!"
—THE LATE, GREAT GOSPEL SINGER ETHEL WATERS

Fact Three: Because God loves me and has a plan for my life, I can choose what type of person I will become: a Victim, a Villain, a Volunteer, or a Victor!

VICTIM: Many of us are the victims of abandonment, betrayal, hurt. These may be from childhood or everyday life; from those close to us or those we meet in the course of life.

VILLAIN: We also have hurt others by our actions or words. We may instill anger in our children because we act as reactors rather than responders. We may keep hurt from healing because we hold on to bitterness. Our own wrong choices cause emotional pain for ourselves and others.

VOLUNTEER: Often, we continue to make poor choices because of a lack of confidence in God and in ourselves or because we allow sin to rule our lives.

VICTOR: The life we want to live is one of victory over the pain of the past, whether it was twenty years ago or yesterday.

This life is possible when I:

- Appropriate the power and love of Christ to forgive and begin again.
- Understand that I am not responsible for the choices of others.

Some of us tend to think that we should have been able to keep a relationship intact "if only" we had done the right things. Have you ever thought, *If only I hadn't said anything. If only I had been prettier. If only I . . . ?* If living a perfect life could keep an offended from the offense, then Jesus would never have been betrayed. But you cannot make a person live the right way or make the right choices. Each of us has our own time of decision.

> Look at the new thing I am going to do. It is already happening. Don't you see it? I will make a road in the desert and rivers in the dry land. (Isaiah 43:18 NCV)

Mom & Mentor Time

Do any of the distortions we just discussed in **Fact One** describe the way you see yourself and/or your situation? What changes could you make in your thought patterns?

Write down any of the self-perceptions mentioned that apply to the way that you think of yourself.

_____

_____

_____

_____

_____

_____

Use **Fact Two** to write about God's perception of you (include that He believes in you, has a personal plan for your life, loves you, etc.). Think about this: *I know God loves me, but what does He like about me?*

List some things:

_____

_____

_____

_____

_____

_____

Which part of this truth is the hardest for you to believe on a daily basis?

_____

_____

_____

_____

_____

_____

GROUP DISCUSSION: Which one of the four are you right now (**Victim, Villain, Volunteer,** or **Victor**)? Which one would you like to be? What has to happen to change you into that person?

face my feelings

Before I can begin to heal, I must fully face my hurt. Before I can forgive, I must identify the hurt. As you think seriously about your hurt, do not deny, spiritualize, or minimize the pain that you experience, whether it involves rejection, neglect, ridicule, criticism, manipulation, or abandonment.

Remember, **unmet needs and hurt emotions turn into personal pain.**

- CIRCLE ANY OF THE FEELINGS YOU EXPERIENCE.

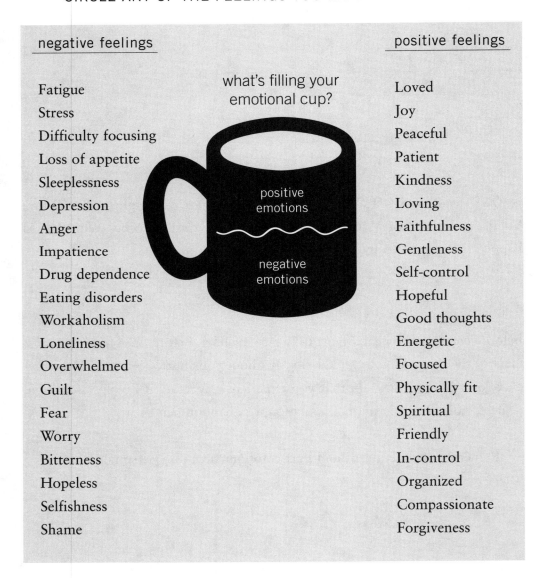

negative feelings		positive feelings
Fatigue	what's filling your emotional cup?	Loved
Stress		Joy
Difficulty focusing		Peaceful
Loss of appetite		Patient
Sleeplessness		Kindness
Depression	positive emotions	Loving
Anger		Faithfulness
Impatience		Gentleness
Drug dependence	negative emotions	Self-control
Eating disorders		Hopeful
Workaholism		Good thoughts
Loneliness		Energetic
Overwhelmed		Focused
Guilt		Physically fit
Fear		Spiritual
Worry		Friendly
Bitterness		In-control
Hopeless		Organized
Selfishness		Compassionate
Shame		Forgiveness

What feeling is most likely to surface when your cup is full?

_____

_____

_____

Draw a horizontal line on the cup diagram to reflect the balance of positive and negative emotions that typically fill your cup.

Where does your line fall? Mostly negative or positive?

_____

Where do you think the negative emotions that overtake your mind are coming from?

_____

_____

_____

_____

_____

Why is your heart grieved? How much of your hurt deals with shame over a particular situation? Who are the people you need to face and with whom you need to work through personal conflict?

_____

_____

_____

_____

_____

Ask yourself: _How does the hurt work as an obstacle to healing in my life? Does it bring depression, discouragement, low self-image?_ Take a moment to think through how this pain of the past is affecting life in the present:

_____

_____

_____

_____

_____

You have just faced some serious pain. Now, let's look at the future! Work through the following exercises with your mentor.

GROUP DISCUSSION: The top four positive emotions I want to develop in the next six weeks are:

1. _____ 2. _____
3. _____ 4. _____

In order for me to do this, I have to:

FOCUS ON THE FACTS. Choose two correct facts and write them.

_____
_____
_____
_____
_____

FACE MY FEELINGS. I need to empty out the negative. Write down the negative thoughts.

_____
_____
_____
_____
_____

USE A POSITIVE WAY OF THINKING. I can put the positive emotions to work in my life by:

Write out at least two sentences about ways to do this.

_____

_____

_____

_____

_____

IMPORTANT ASSIGNMENT: This week, write a letter to the person or persons who have betrayed or hurt you. Explain the pain you feel and acknowledge that you understand that person (or persons) has his or her own pain to deal with. Use this lesson to help you write this therapeutic letter. Emphasize the importance, and possibly the difficulty of, writing this letter(s). This lesson is for your emotional benefit, and **it need not ever be sent.** Sometimes we don't even recognize how deeply something has impacted us until we write it down. **This homework is essential because next week we will build on it.**

One key to emptying emotional pain is praying for others. Before you leave, write down the name of at least two people in the room you can pray for this week. Put the information in your workbook.

_____

_____

healing emotional pain—part II

Let's review: Healing can freely occur when I . . .

Focus on the Facts

- God is on my side.
- I can choose the kind of person I will become.

Face My Feelings

- Why am I angry, hurt, ashamed, and disappointed?
- What emotions do I want to fill my life?

We must now **Feed Our Faith** and **Forgive Our Foes.**

> Now He was teaching in one of the synagogues on the
> Sabbath. And behold, there was a woman who had a spirit of
> infirmity eighteen years, and was bent over and could in no
> way raise herself up. But when Jesus saw her, He called her

to Him and said to her, "Woman, you are loosed from your infirmity." And He laid His hands on her, and immediately she was made straight, and glorified God. (Luke 13:10–13)

feed my faith

This woman was bound over, not by a physical disease, but by a sickness caused by "a spirit." Hers was an emotional and spiritual bondage that had gone on for eighteen years and resulted in complete crippling: "She was bent over and could in no way raise herself up" (v. 11). Notice that she was doing the right things; she was in the synagogue on the Sabbath. Even in a place of worship, she found herself to be powerless, but then she met Christ personally. Jesus called her and she responded. He touched her, and she was healed. How do we know? Because she stood up! No longer did she see dust and dirt, but then she was able to see love in the eyes of another and the beauty of God's creation. She chose a new view of life. She began glorifying God with words of faith.

A changed heart is possible because:

SALVATION is exclusive. Only God can do it.
SALVATION is extensive. All things are made new.
SALVATION is the chance to live again by faith.

Now faith is the substance of things hoped for, the evidence of things not seen. (Hebrews 11:1)

Your faith is not standing by to use only in case of emergency. It is an everyday faith for everyday living. Are you having trouble believing? In Mark 9, a father brought his child to Jesus for healing, and Jesus challenged the man to believe. "Immediately the father of the child cried out, and said with tears, 'Lord, I believe; help my unbelief!'" (v. 24). And Jesus healed that child. He did not say, "You don't believe enough." He understood the man's desire to have faith and answered his prayer. When we come to Him expecting an answer, He will give us the faith to go on—and He will heal.

We must believe His Word and His love—cling to it, rely on it, trust in Him!

believe God is who He says He is

- The unconditional lover of my soul—What can separate us from the love of Christ? Nothing! (See Romans 8:35)
- All-powerful—God can do exceedingly more than we could ask or imagine. (See Ephesians 3:20)
- He holds my times in His hands—"My times are in Your hand" (Psalm 31:15).

rehearse what He has already done and praise Him for it

Has He blessed you and your children? Has He gotten you through difficulties? Then relive those times over and over in your mind, thank Him, rejoice in that He will do it again and again for you. And if that gets too hard, read the miracles found in God's Word! He did it for them, He will surely do it for you!

Now that you have focused on the facts, faced your feelings, and made the decision to feed your faith, it is time to set yourself free to:

forgive your foes

Forgiveness IS:

- an illogical response to behavior that deserves punishment;
- setting us free to experience joy, peace, and contentment;
- a choice, one that Jesus made from the beginning.

Forgiveness IS NOT:

- acting like it didn't happen;
- excusing the wrong like it was an accident;
- always going to result in reconciliation;
- the same as trusting the person again.

Forgiveness IS:

- healing power for the offended and the offender;
- an act of great strength and will;
- a commandment of God.

Jesus prayed: "And forgive us our debts, As we forgive our debtors" (Matthew 6:12). These two phrases are directly connected. I cannot enjoy the freedom of being forgiven if I do not freely forgive.

> *"To forgive those seeking to injure you*
> *is to remove yourself from their control"*
> —JACK HAYFORD

Now, as we speak, a person's face is popping into your head. Freedom, ladies! Choose this freedom to love again, to believe in the best for yourself and your children, and to no longer allow the actions of others to rule your heart.

Certainly forgiveness is grace, unearned and undeserved. Jesus made a choice to forgive His offenders. On the cross, with His last breaths He said, "Father, forgive them, for they do not know what they do" (Luke 23:34). We need to remember that offenders do not know what they do. They are as misguided today as when they sent an innocent, loving Jesus to the cross.

For Jesus, certainly, Judas, the soldiers who beat Him, and those who hated Him were part of His prayer. Consider for a moment what He must have felt—shame, humiliation, physical pain, separation from loved ones, betrayal. Based on these Scriptures, do you think our Lord understands your emotional pain? As He hung bleeding and beaten, Jesus most certainly did not rely on feelings to enable His choice to forgive. No, it was a pure act of the will, the canceling of a debt, a choice reflecting the unsurpassed love of God.

Imagine with me for a moment that you are holding your anger, bitterness, and disappointment regarding one specific person or event in your hands. Clench both fists tightly and punch them out in front of you. Now, slowly, deliberately open your hands and release those negative emotions. Let them leave and feel them leaving. Shake your hands out if you need to, and open them more than once. Then bring those open hands back to your heart. Repeat this every day if you want, or any time you need to "let go" of negative emotions.

> *"Total forgiveness is choosing to send away*
> *destructive, past memories and*
> *beginning life again fresh and new."*
>
> —JAY STRACK

Remember Jay's story of salvation? Some twenty years later, Jay and his Dad met to talk in the Florida Keys. Please allow me to share more of his story:

Finally, I was face to face with my dad. He was a like a stranger to me, but I believed that God wanted me to forgive him. Looking at my Dad for the first time in years, I could feel the root of bitterness beginning to loosen its stronghold inside me. I wondered if maybe he too hadn't been the victim of a hopeless past. I studied his face, wondering, "How could you not have cared about your own son?" Questions poured out of me as though a retaining wall had suddenly given way. I wanted to know about his leaving . . . his apparent lack of concern . . . the letters he never answered.

Dad looked at me—I mean for the first time I can remember, he really looked at me. I saw the pain on his face. "Jay, I never got any of those letters. I never knew."

I learned quite a few lessons that night—for example, that there are three sides to every story: your side, the other side, and the true side. But most of all, I realized that this man had never intended to destroy me; he had been on his own trip of self-destruction. Alcohol consumed him; he had only vague memories of those days when I needed him so badly.

As the tide washed in and out, I felt a great sense of peace bathing my soul. An unexpected lifting of the heavy bitterness revealed a new heart in me. At last I understood. It wasn't anything I'd done wrong. It wasn't that Dad hadn't loved me, either. He had drowned in his own problems and alcohol addiction.

I chose that night to forgive him and to move toward a fresh start. I couldn't begin with a father-son relationship, but friendship developed, and eventually so did bonds of family. It was my joy to discuss the power of God's salvation and a new start with my dad, and on the night before his death, pray over him with complete forgiveness. It is a moment I will never forget.

Won't you make the choice today to send away destruction and begin anew? If you go back to Isaac and Ishmael, you see that this jealously and resentment created a hate that has no parallel in history. This hatred has continuously set off wars and atrocities for some four thousand years. And it is the title deed to the land of Israel, which God promised to Abraham's lineage, that has been the source of the friction between the Jews and the Arabs right up to this very moment. Every day you see the result of Sarah's decision and the bitterness that Hagar passed to Ishmael.

Every choice carries with it a consequence or a blessing. The choice to forgive can result in the freedom to soar to new heights, to make new relationships, to feel good about yourself, and to believe in the plans God has for you and for your children.

As we close, I must ask you a question. If your children do not find peace and learn forgiveness in your home, where will they find it? Not on the school grounds, not in the workplace. No, they need to learn it from you, mom. Give them this great gift of freedom through forgiveness, and they will hold it in their hearts forever.

GROUP DISCUSSION

COMMON RESISTANCES	RELATED REFLECTIONS
The offender hasn't asked for forgiveness.	"Vengeance is mine," says the Lord.
The offender hasn't "changed."	Forgiveness is for my benefit—don't wait!
The offender doesn't "deserve" forgiveness.	Forgiving at this point is primarily a choice, *not* a feeling; feeling grateful for God's love and forgiveness of me encourages this choice.
Punishment is appropriate, and I'm going to be the one to do it.	What if God had waited for me to change before forgiving me?
It's my right to hold a grudge.	Who truly does "deserve" forgiveness?
I'll forgive whenever I feel like it.	Holding grudges hurts me, *not* the offender.

Every one of us has varying degrees of pain in our past. To "shake off the dust" of the past requires us to **A-C-T** out a plan.

A—**Admit that anger and bitterness are controlling you,** coloring your picture of life, and inflicting more pain.

C—**Choose to forgive the offenses.** This choice is in solely your power and must be a conscious act of your will.

T—**Toss away your tendency to obsessively dwell upon the offensive memories.** You cannot deny them, but you can decide to minimize their power over your mind.

Therefore, if anyone is in Christ, he is a new creation; old things have passed away; behold all things have become new. (2 Corinthians 5:17)

FORGIVENESS BLESSES ME!
- I can enjoy new relationships and restore old ones.
- I can trust again.
- I am no longer controlled by a person or the past.
- I become physically healthy.
- I become emotionally healthy.
- I am filled with joy and hope for the future.
- It empowers me to move forward with confidence.
- I can grow in intimacy with God. I can remove destructive, negative thoughts from my mind.

WRITE A THERAPEUTIC LETTER.

Step One: Who do I need to forgive? _____

Step Two: Use the **A-C-T** outline to control your thought process as you write.

This may seem difficult at first, but the benefit is freedom, healing, and a great peace that will fuel you right into the future and bless your children with joy.

five
breaking the pain cycle for your children

Do you ever walk through the mall by yourself, only to turn at the first call of "Mom!"? I can't walk through a church without smiling at a child, wiping a nose, or helping a child up. When my kids walk in the door, my first thought is to hug them and ask what I can do for them. It's just *in* me—being a mom. All kids need moms, but most importantly, all kids need healthy, holy moms. There is no substitute for the heart of a mother. There is nothing more important; nothing of more value; nothing as lasting as investing carefully and deliberately in your children. There may be many things you want to do; many things you wonder about doing; many things you will try to do; but there is **one thing you must do—be an emotionally and spiritually healthy mother!**

Children and teens should not have to emotionally process or shoulder your angry, bitter emotions or the resulting poison they leave in their wake. You have been a **Victim**, you have been a **Villain**, perhaps even a **Volunteer**. Now it is time to show your children what a **Victor** looks like. Not only can you stop toxic family members and offenders from poisoning your well of life; you must begin *today* to leave a heritage for your children.

Paul gave us pure therapy for anyone who is ready to break the cycle of pain.

> If anyone is in Christ, he is a new creation; old things have
> passed away; behold, all things have become new.
> (2 Corinthians 5:17)

Three important truths are found in this verse. **Through Christ, I have:**

1. **A new position in life:** I am part of a new family, I am in the family of God.
2. **A new personality:** I don't have to be a screamer or a hysterical parent with out-of-control emotions. People say, "My mother was this way. I can't help it." Yes, it is true that we are deeply impacted by both the successes and failures of our parents, but there comes a time when we must grow up emotionally. We can no longer use their actions as a reason for our inability to break the pattern. Christ can and will help me to become a peaceful, godly woman.
3. **A new potential:** I realize that, if I want to, I can break free from the bondage that is holding me back.

Clearly, God has outlined in His Word a choice for each of us. Second Corinthians 5:17 uses important language:

- If *anyone*—that would be you and me.
- *All* things have become *NEW*—so we have to quit dragging out the old emotions! God has given us new ones to use, and we must use them.

Rahab was a young woman whose life didn't start off well. In fact, Joshua 2 tells us that she was a prostitute. The spies sent by Joshua came to her inn, and she helped them. Why? Even though this pagan woman had heard only second-hand of the great Jehovah God, she chose to believe. Here is her declaration of faith:

> For we have heard how the LORD dried up the water of the Red
> Sea for you when you came out of Egypt, and what you did to
> the two kings of the Amorites who were on the other side of
> the Jordan, Sihon and Og, whom you utterly destroyed. And as
> soon as we heard these things, our hearts melted; neither did
> there remain any more courage in anyone because of you, for
> the LORD your God, He is God in heaven above and on earth
> beneath. (Joshua 2:10–11)

Rahab decided to risk her life by trusting God and helping the spies. In return, they saved her life and the lives of her family. It is a dramatic story you must read. But perhaps the most important aspect of the story is that God doesn't care where we start or what we've done. Remember our verse:

> The LORD says, "Forget about what happened before, and do
> not think about the past. Look at the new thing I am going to
> do. It is already happening." (Isaiah 43:18–19 NCV)

You might be having trouble believing that God is serious about this forgetting the past thing, but He is. I have read it over and over, but to me the story of Rahab is one of the most powerful. Read on:

> The book of the genealogy of Jesus Christ, the Son of David,
> the Son of Abraham: Abraham begot Isaac, Isaac begot Jacob,

and Jacob begot Judah and his brothers . . . Salmon begot
Boaz by Rahab, Boaz begot Obed by Ruth, Obed begot Jesse,
and Jesse begot David the king. . . . And Matthan begot
Jacob. And Jacob begot Joseph the husband of Mary, of whom
was born Jesus who is called Christ. (Matthew 1:1–6, 15–16)

Now I have skipped over a few generations, but the story is clear: Rahab started out a prostitute, but her decision to live by faith changed everything. So much so that God was able to place her in the line of the Messiah! What a lovely picture of God's grace. He not only gave her a new position, a new personality, and a new potential, but her dramatic salvation is a story handed down over thousands of years from generation to generation, and it will continue to be told. And this story of the grace of God is one of hope and mercy for each of us.

All things have become new. We cannot continue to drag out the old emotions! God has given us new ones to use and we must use them. Ask yourself: *Why am I the way I am when I could be the way Christ wants me to be?* You must become healthy so that you can raise emotionally healthy children.

Jay Strack says, "Conflict between kids and their parents begins when parents fail to live up to the standard they have established for the family." For example, you want your child to keep her word, but when you break a promise the child is told, "You just have to understand." You want him or her to make the best choices without following what others say, yet you may be making choices based on what you think others say about you. You may tell your child not to compare what other families do to what your family does, but then you voice a negative comparison. Choose your words wisely.

These double-minded acts are the sparks of a chain reaction leading to a crisis of rebellion. The majority of rebellions begin with hurt feelings over something the parents have said or done. Although neither side meant to hurt the other, significant damage can occur. The parent probably will walk away, be angry, and then let it go, but the child may harbor that hurt and allow it to turn into bitterness, affecting his or her own spiritual life in the process. Some teens can tell you the exact time, day, and place of an incident with their parents. With detail they describe the pain that led them to reject their own families, whether one incident or a chain of incidents. Hurt harbored in the heart soon becomes bitterness, and ultimately, rebellion.

Understanding that anger can lead to disruptive behavior brings a mother to the next question. How do I discipline the child in a way that will correct the problem? The answer lies in communication and understanding.

Be sure to choose *correction* over punishment: *response* over reaction.

If I **react** to my child's behavior, then I am hurt, embarrassed, angry, etc.

If I **respond** to my child's behavior, then I want to find out why it happened, what need is unmet, and what I can do to correct the attitude and resulting action.

> A soft answer turns away wrath, But a harsh word stirs up
> anger. (Proverbs 15:1)

When we understand the value of a mother's heart, we look at every conflict as an opportunity for understanding our children. When we are emotionally healthy, we can respond to our child's behavior in order to make correction. Your mentor is going to work through some parenting tips with you. I want you to begin thanking the Lord every day for the wonderful work He is going to do through your child. Ask Him to bless you as a mother and to bless your family. Remember, He intensely loves you and wants the best for your life. Dare to ask Him for it!

CORRECTION OVER PUNISHMENT: RESPONSE OVER REACTION

AS A PARENT	CORRECTION	PUNISHMENT
My goal is:	To develop responsibility	*NOT* to get even
My motivation is:	Love, concern for the effect of misbehavior on my child	*NOT* frustration, hostility, rejection of my child
My emphasis is:	A changed heart toward the current offense through personal understanding of it.	*NOT* past mistakes/choices
I want my child's apology:	To be genuine repentance, security, and gratitude	*NOT* anger, condemnation, and fear
I want my child to see God:	As One who loves and protects	*NOT* as One who seeks to punish

Using the chart that follows, identify the most significant needs of your children, and write their initials by each. Then discuss how to meet those needs. If you are having difficulty, try describing a child's problematic behavior, then brainstorm about what some of the underlying emotional needs might be.

accepted	confident	in control	reassured
accepting	developed	included	recognized
accomplished	educated	independent	relaxed
acknowledged	empowered	interested	respected
admired	enouragement	knowledgeable	safe
affection	focused	listened to	satisfied
alive	forgiven	loved	secure
amused	forgiving	needed	significant
appreciated	free	noticed	successful
appreciative	fulfilled	open	supported
approved of	grown or growing	optimistic	treated fairly
attention	happy	powerful	understanding
capable	heard	privacy	understood
challenged	helped	productive	useful
clear (not confused)	helpful	protected	valued
comfort	important	proud	worthy
competent			

My Child	His or Her Top Needs	What I Can Do To Meet These Needs
_____	_____	_____
_____	_____	_____
_____	_____	_____
_____	_____	_____

My Child	His or Her Top Needs	What I Can Do To Meet These Needs
_____	_____	_____
_____	_____	_____
_____	_____	_____
_____	_____	_____

My Child	His or Her Top Needs	What I Can Do To Meet These Needs
_____	_____	_____
_____	_____	_____
_____	_____	_____

My Child	His or Her Top Needs	What I Can Do To Meet These Needs
_____	_____	_____
_____	_____	_____
_____	_____	_____

Were any of your priority needs the same as your children's? What were they?

_____

_____

_____

_____

_____

_____

Do you think that any of your own negative emotions spill over into your relationship with your children? Name a specific way this happens.

_____

_____

_____

_____

_____

_____

Choose one priority need for each child. How can you meet that need to solve a current problem or encourage good behavior in your child?

_____

_____

_____

_____

_____

_____

How would these interactions be different if you focus on meeting needs rather than only on addressing behavior?

_____

_____

_____

_____

_____

_____

additional resource notes

Most likely, you have watched your children become angry and hold that anger in. He or she can become as frustrated as you are and can pick up on your every stress as well. From *Parenting With Intimacy* by Dr. David Ferguson:

HOW TO HELP YOUR CHILD PROCESS AND DISPEL ANGER:

A—Acknowledge the child's anger.
I can tell you're really angry.
It looks like you're very mad.
I can see that you're upset.
Your face tells me that you're feeling angry.

N—Notice who and what the anger is about; then express this to the angry child.

You're angry at your brother for taking your toy.

You're angry at your friends for leaving you out.

You are angry at me and/or your father for not being together.

You are angry because our family has changed.

G—Get to the deeper, "tender" emotions.

I am wondering if you are feeling _____ as well as feeling angry.

(For example: hurt, disappointment, embarrassment, rejection, loneliness, insecurity, anxiousness, etc.)

E—Express care.

I really wish that your brother had not done that to you. It really hurts when someone takes something that belongs to you.

I am sad for you that your friends put you down. I know that must have hurt, especially because of your special friendship.

I am sorry that being a divorced or single-parent family is difficult and may feel different to you. It is sometimes difficult for me. Do you feel afraid, abandoned, lonely, and angry about it?

R—Respond wisely and pray together.

Dear God, thank You for beginning to heal the painful emotions in my cup. You know I was angry about _____. I am choosing to forgive _____ today because You have forgiven me. I choose to let go of my anger. I choose to cancel that person's debt. I pray that You would continue to help me get rid of my anger. In Jesus' name, amen.

six
listening and communicating as a family

Susanna Wesley gave birth to nineteen children in nineteen years. Her husband was a poor money manager, and, at times, he was tyrannical at home. Once, after a minor disagreement, he abandoned Susanna and their several children for an entire year. No matter what the circumstances, Susanna was committed to caring for her family the best way possible.

Though resources were limited, she started a daily school for her children. Each day before class, she set aside an hour to herself for Scripture reading and prayer, and then led them all in singing psalms. Because Susanna wanted to develop a personal relationship with each child, she scheduled a private appointment with each of them once a week for encouragement. These bonds of faith and love helped them survive continual hardships.

She lived just long enough to see the fruits of her work. Two months before she died in July 1742, her son John preached a series of revival messages in their hometown of Epworth, England, to the biggest crowds that area had ever seen. John Wesley is the founder of Methodism. His brother Charles wrote more than nine thousand hymns and poems, many of which are still sung today. Susanna

Wesley said her purpose was exclusively the saving of her children's souls, and she accomplished that for her children and more.

Think of your own life: Has being able to talk out your life and have someone listen with compassion been helpful and beneficial to you? It has been said that a great deal of behavioral problems come from children wanting adults to listen to them. Don't just assume the kids are happy. Ask questions, listen for clues, and find out exactly what is going through their minds and hearts. Children are also vulnerable to the pressures a parent faces through divorce, abandonment, financial difficulties, and emotional stresses. Ask yourself, *What can I do to foster an environment that would be more conducive to open communication?*

As with other emotional needs, the need to be heard is a survival need. By developing our own listening skills, we can model them to our children. In turn, they will become better listeners, and we will feel heard, understood, and respected.

COMMUNICATION: Most of us know that there are four "C's" that determine the value or final cost of a diamond. These same words can be used to determine the value of your family communication when applied. For example:

- **Carat**—The size of the diamond = The size of the issue or goal of the communication
- **Color**—The way it reflects light = **Respond** or **React** and the "coloring" of attitudes
- **Clarity**—How clear a diamond is = A clear understanding between parents and children
- **Cut**—The specific look to a diamond = What is the goal? What exactly do you want your family to become as you carefully polish the edges?

Carat—This represents the size of the issue or goal. Not every situation is major. It has been said that a parent must pick her battles. For example, messy rooms are not addressed in the same manner as using profanity; not doing homework is different than disrespect. All must be addressed, but with an eye for the cause, not the symptom.

> And Jesus increased in wisdom and stature, and in favor with
> God and men. (Luke 2:52)

Color—The word *bitterness* literally comes from the word for *dye* and means "to color." You must ask yourself what things in your past or even in the present might be "coloring" this issue or intensifying it. Mothers set the tone, but they also react quickly to it. Communication often breaks down because the child no longer feels confident about opening up to parents. He or she fears being hurt again and, therefore, keeps feelings and frustrations inside, leading to a loss of love and respect. Be sure to use the **Respond vs. React** rule.

> Pursue peace with all people, and holiness, without which no
> one will see the Lord. (Hebrews 12:14)

Clarity—How clearly do I communicate the essential elements of the discussion? Can I remove enough emotion in order to see the cause of the problem, or am I only seeing the symptom? Am I explaining the offense with the understanding of correction and teaching rather than with anger, blame, and punishment? Am I allowing my child to fully express how he or she feels, or am I afraid of the discussion? A child should be able to ask or say anything without feeling rejected, laughed at, or unimportant.

A soft answer turns away wrath, But a harsh word stirs up
anger. (Proverbs 15:1)

Cut—Be clear on what the outcome of this communication needs to be.
What is the final goal: understanding, correction, repentance, a stronger relationship? Power, control, a transfer of anger, a broken spirit? Contrary to some
argument patterns you may have experienced, no one needs to be the "winner."
When we understand each other and come to an agreement on how to move
forward, everyone wins.

He who keeps instruction is in the way of life, But he who
refuses correction goes astray. (Proverbs 10:17)

These four "C's" come together and determine the final cost of a diamond.

Cost—Family communication may cost you more patience, time, and mercy
than you think you have, but the value of the outcome can never be measured
with dollars. Is it worth it? You bet it is.

A **Family Mission Statement** is the foundation of clear communication, but, as
the leader, you must first feel confident about your personal mission statement.
In a few minutes you will work with your mentor to begin a mission statement.
You can choose from the sample values on the page in your workbook and add
others that are also important to you. Begin by circling six to ten values or biblical principles from the list below to get started. Choose what is most valuable
to you.

SAMPLE VALUES: Choose from these sample values or add your own.

Adventure	Beauty	Career	Compassion
Contribution	Courage	Creativity	Education
Excellence	Faith	Family	Faithful
Generous	Good Attitude	Financial Security	Gratitude
Growth	Humor	Honesty	Humility
Innovation	Inspiration	Joy	Leadership
Love	Loyalty	Obedient	Patience
Peace	Respect	Servant-Hearted	Spiritual
Success	Team Player	Tenacious	Willing Hearted
Work Ethic			

After you choose your values, write in the roles in your life: mother, employee, neighbor, friend, sister, daughter, athlete, artist, and so on. Those values plus the roles in your life will equal your mission statement.

My Roles: _____ _____ _____

_____ _____ _____

Values + Roles = My Life Purpose

Write two to three sentences describing yourself using the **Values + Roles** recipe for life purpose (see page 74 for an example).

_____

_____

_____

_____

_____

_____

_____

_____

_____

For example: *I am a patient, compassionate mother who instills courage, faith, and gratitude in her children. I am successful as a team player in my career because of my willing heart, servant attitude, and work ethic. I am faithful to the Lord in devotion and service because He has been faithful to me. I love my church and seek to serve within it as well as develop friendships and fellowship. As a friend, I work hard to love others. Personally, I seek peace, joy, and inspiration through reading the Word of God, hearing it taught, and choosing positive friendships.*

Later during the week, as you introduce this concept to your children, help them choose values and write down roles. As you help them make a mission statement, you can combine theirs with yours to make a Family Mission Statement. Hang this prominently in the house as a constant reminder of what your family stands for. It's fun and builds great communication.

In the end, the goal is a celebration of your family—a definition of who you are and what you stand for that your children can be proud of and hold on to. This will go a long way toward your children's self-esteem and confidence and will encourage love in the family.

the family meeting

Family Meetings give families an opportunity to create traditions, resolve issues, review goals, make long-range plans, applaud accomplishments, build self-esteem and self-reliance in children, simplify and organize family matters, and promote important values such as character development, mutual love and respect, and community responsibility and awareness. They build memories that last a lifetime and bonds that grow into adulthood.

The Rules and Tools of a Family Meeting

1. Have fun! At every meeting, celebrate who you are as a family. Be grateful for one another and tell each other so. Make every meeting a pep rally for each member of the family and a safe place for children to speak, think, ask, and listen.

2. Have the meeting on the same day at the and same time, if possible, each week or every other week as your household schedule permits. By doing this, everyone will be able to plan around that special time. Keep it on a wall calendar prominently displayed in the kitchen or family room and let everyone know how sacred this time is. Once your children see how important it is to you, it will become important to them. Unplug phones, pagers, faxes, or anything that beeps!

   Occasionally, you may need to reschedule or shorten the meeting. Do so joyfully, always keeping the meeting as a tool for communication and an enjoyable time.

3. Keep the mood light and fun, except for the serious discussions that need to occur. Start with a game, a craft project, or a song. Be sure you choose age-appropriate games and time them to be relatively short at first. The time spent will grow because the children will enjoy it, especially when they are encouraged to express themselves and are recognized and appreciated.

4. Elect a new moderator-leader at every meeting so that every person feels equally important and a part of the meeting. This is not a "Mom says" time, but a time to discuss family needs, make goals together, and dream about the future. Also elect a secretary to take notes each week.

5. Consider assigning brief reading in magazines, books, or newspapers, and let children "report" on what they learned and how they feel about it. Keep the ages of the children in mind as you plan.

6. Keep a calendar in the middle of the table to note who has a test this week, sports, appointments, church, work, school, or any other significant events. This immediately tells each child that he or she is important as each person makes a note of the date and time and promises to pray.

7. Every meeting doesn't have to have a tidy ending. It's a place of discussion, and if the family cannot come to a consensus on a problem, then ask everyone to pray about it until the next meeting. This teaches prayer and faith.

8. Be prepared to share verses, give out minutes of the previous meeting, agendas, goals, ideas, and "homework."

9. Begin with positive remarks: "I appreciate the way you kept your room this week. I had so much fun being with you yesterday. I liked watching you try hard at sports, it made be proud to be your mom. I love your (smile, joy, attitude, etc.). I am grateful for you because . . . God has blessed me by . . ." Be sure that every child says "thank you" after the compliment and thoroughly receives the praise. These are deposits in the emotional bank that can never be robbed or taken away.

10. Approach problem-solving as a "who has an idea" game. Always use principles and absolutes to solve the problem but listen to all the ideas. In the end the answer usually becomes apparent. Keep asking questions and let everyone answer.

11. Keep a "suggestion box" or agenda list on the refrigerator so that each person can add things they want to talk about.

12. The leader should be prepared to end the meeting with a Scripture (you can help with this during the week) and some fun surprise like a snack, a game, or a song.

13. Be patient. It may take time for older children to become involved.

Check our Web site at www.newstart4moms.org for family fun ideas and recipes and other links to family games and crafts.

seven

praying powerful prayers for your children

She watches over the ways of her household, And does not eat the bread of idleness. Her children rise up and call her blessed. . . . Charm is deceitful and beauty is passing, But a woman who fears the LORD, she shall be praised.
(Proverbs 31:27, 28a, 30)

What do you suppose God wants to do with your child? Will you be there to help him or her stay focused? I hope that you were able to sit down together and write a Family Mission Statement and that you are excited about God using you as a mother to raise godly, successful children.

Let's go over a few basic parenting rules that you can build on:

- As part of your meeting times together, **always set high standards for yourself and your family.** Being a single-parent family never means being a second-class family. Let your children know the value of honesty, hard work, and faith in God. Expect them to live up to it and they will. This does not mean you can choose their goals for them. But it does mean that together you can choose and set values to live by and hold each other to those values.

- **Never lie, ever.** Be honest with your kids. They know when you tell them "half-truths," but don't be brutal. Say everything to yourself before you say it to them and ask, *How did that make me feel?*
- **Do what is right. It's never right to do wrong and never wrong to do right.** If it means saying "I'm sorry," do it. If it means forgiving an offender who doesn't care, do it. If it means going without to help someone else, or working extra hours to do the job with excellence, do it. Remember that children will always follow your example, both good and bad.
- **It's not important WHO is right, but WHAT is right.** This rule ends many sibling rivalries.
- **Be involved in each other's lives.** Moms should get to know teachers and ask about behavior before it becomes a problem. Know the friends your kids hang with, and make your house the place to be so you know what is going on and who is who. Ask your kids on a regular basis about their day and week, and share information on yours.
- **Establish intimacy with your children by consistently praying together.** Pray for each other's needs, for the family needs, and for the needs of others. Confess sins against one another, and give thanks to God for His goodness.

PRAYING FOR MY CHILDREN is the greatest gift I can give them. It is my highest honor as a mom. God's intention is to use you as a godly mother in the lives of your children. While we argue and cry over every petty thing, we are losing the battle for our children, mainly because we are fighting the wrong enemy.

> For we do not wrestle against flesh and blood, but against
> principalities, against powers, against the rulers of darkness of
> this age. (Ephesians 6:12)

You must believe that being a prayer warrior is your greatest work as a parent. As parents, we tend to feel it is all up to us, but God reminds us that through prayer and our consistent example, He will do the work. Be sure not to pray over and over for the one character flaw or the change in your child that you believe needs to be made. Pray instead for the whole child, for every area of life. As the whole healing and strengthening takes place, that particular area will take care of itself.

> Arise, cry out in the night, At the beginning of the watches;
> Pour out your heart like water before the face of the Lord. Lift
> your hands toward Him For the life of your young children.
> (Lamentations 2:19)

For many children, the burden of approaching adulthood and the everyday stresses of life are more than they can bear. As independence for the child approaches, the need to intercede in prayer increases. But *how* do you pray effectively for your children?

> For this reason we also, since the day we heard it, do not
> cease to pray for you, and to ask that you may be filled with
> knowledge of His will in all wisdom and spiritual understand-
> ing; that you may walk worthy of the Lord, fully pleasing Him,
> being fruitful in every good work and increasing in the knowl-
> edge of God; strengthened with all might, according to His

glorious power, for all patience and longsuffering with joy.
(Colossians 1:9–11)

Paul, inspired by the Holy Spirit, told us exactly how and what to pray in
Colossians 1:9–11.

- **Do not cease to pray** (v 9). Consistent, sincere prayer that grows with
  the child. What is a good time for you to set aside to pray earnestly for
  your children—early in the morning, before bed, or during the day? Set
  a time, plan it daily, and keep a prayer journal or a notebook in the
  same spot so that you can record both requests and answers. It can be
  ten minutes or an hour or short prayers throughout the day. The key is
  consistency and faith.
- **That you may be filled** (v 9). We want our children to experience
  nothing less than the abundant life Jesus promised in John 10:10: "I
  have come that they may have life, and that they may have it more
  abundantly." Kids are looking for fun but often complain of boredom.
  Pray that they will enjoy life and learn the value of simple pleasures
  without being addicted to wastefulness.
- **With the knowledge of His will** (v 9). To be headed in the right
  direction, every person must know the individual plan and
  purpose of God. Pray that your children will seek God's best and
  that the experiences of growing years will act to establish good
  habits.
- **In all wisdom** (v 9). Pray that the Lord will place people into your
  children's lives who will show them good examples and act as a good
  influence, not only godly friends but also worthy heroes. This wisdom
  Paul speaks of is the knowledge of first principles, the foundation of

mental excellence. Pray for the ability to learn, and to have good study skills and habits, good memory, and an excellent relationship with teachers.

- **Spiritual understanding** (v 9). Pray for your children to begin to develop spiritual independence so that they will make the transfer from mom's faith to their own *genuine* faith. Although this begins at salvation, we want to continue to pray for spiritual growth in each life. Pray that the truth and teachings of Scripture will move from their heads to their hearts. Use Scripture memorization as a family fun time—sing Bible verses, draw them, teach the children to love the Word of God. Try www.family.org, the Web site of Focus on the Family, for simple, fun games that teach biblical principles.

- **That you may walk worthy** (v 10). The walk described here is one of total conduct in the course of life, a decision of the heart to walk in the will of God as taught to the child using the Scriptures. Here we pray for responsibility, morality, the understanding of right and wrong, and the overcoming of temptation. Pray for the Lord to send a godly couple into your lives with whom your children can interact and learn from, as well as other friends they can look to as examples. Be sure you bring positive people into their lives, people of faith who live strong during difficult days. These everyday lessons that are "caught" rather than taught can be most powerful. Never hesitate to ask for help. The worst that can happen is they say "no," but it will only be to protect you as God answers your prayers. Trust Him to bring the right friends into your lives as a family.

- **Fully pleasing Him** (v 10). Pray for your child to develop as a servant leader. Help him or her find a meaningful service and a love for the church so that they might receive the blessing of serving. When children learn to serve, they learn to relate rightly to other people. The summer is a great time to teach "time tithing." In this activity, children are to "tithe" by giving away 10 percent of their time throughout the summer to a charitable act of their choice. It might be cleaning a neighbor's house, babysitting someone's children for free, or visiting people at a nursing home, etc. Invite the children to be creative in their choices, but be sure that they understand the key truth of the activity: the only joy in life is found in that which we give away. Creating purpose in your child banishes boredom from the present and peaceful habits for the future.

- **Being fruitful in every good work** (v 10). Pray for your child to be successful in his or her endeavors, not to necessarily win every game or score high on every test, but to find an area of life that he or she enjoys doing and does well. A child whose self-esteem is smashed over failure will be an adult whose self-esteem is easily destroyed. Teach them to learn something good from every failure and encourage them to keep trying new things. Don't hesitate to share your failures with your child honestly, but be sure to also share what you learned from it, how you moved forward, etc.

- **Increasing in the knowledge of God** (v 10). To help them understand God's holiness, explain that He hates sin but loves the sinner. This is a good time to explain that you love your children very much and will never stop loving them, but you do not love it when they disobey or make wrong choices.

- **Strengthened with all might** (v 11). Praying for protection is important, but too often we forget to pray for strength. You cannot always be present as they battle temptations, but you can be present in spirit by praying through Ephesians 6:13–17 with them in mind. I have several friends who tell me they have always prayed, "Lord, see where I can't.

Be there to bring my child through when I am not." We want them to begin to make their own correct choices, to win over temptation by saying "yes" to God's best.

- **For all patience** (v 11). This may seem a contradiction in terms for any child or teen who can't wait to grow up. Ask a child how old he or she is and you are likely to get the number at the next birthday with "I will be" or "I'm almost." The kind of patience Paul prays for here is patience with people, the capacity to get along with difficult people who might try to crush a child's spirit. Pray for the ability to deal with the unlovely without becoming irritated, without bitterness, and without retaliation; for example, with a bully on the playground, a teacher-student relationship, or peer pressure.

- **Longsuffering with joy** (v 11). This is a picture of turning burdens into glory, of a prayer for self-restraint and even-temperedness on a consistent basis and with joy.

Every child has to take his or her own path to independence. For some, it will be a straight path with no crooked turns, for others it will be an occasional stray off the path, and for a few there may even be hairpin turns! That is what happened to the disciple Peter as he grew spiritually: he walked with the Lord, then denied Him three times. In the end he wrote a book of the New Testament, started churches, and eventually died a martyr for Christ. Here is what Jesus said to Peter:

> Simon, Simon, Satan has asked to test all of you as a farmer
> sifts his wheat. I have prayed that you will not lose your faith!
> Help your brothers be stronger when you come back to me.
> (Luke 22:31–32 NCV)

Peter came back strong and influenced many others for the gospel. What a great example of the importance and power of prayer in a life as children grow! What counts is that through each learning lesson they grow wiser and stronger, and eventually walk right into a spirit-filled life. Your prayers can make that difference. Do you believe it?

GOD CAN DO IT! GOD CAN DO IT THROUGH YOU!

changing thought patterns

> And he (Elkanah) had two wives . . . Peninnah had
> children, but Hannah had no children. . . . And her rival
> also provoked her severely, to make her miserable, because
> the LORD had closed her womb. So it was, year by year,
> when she went up to the house of the LORD, that she
> provoked her; therefore she (Hannah) wept and did not
> eat. . . . And she was in bitterness of soul, and prayed to
> the Lord and wept in anguish. (1 Samuel 1:2, 6–7, 10)

Day after day, Hannah listened to the snickers and snide remarks: "You can't give your husband a child. I already did! What kind of woman are you?" She lived in a society that marked a woman's value by the number of children, especially sons, she was able to give her husband. The peer pressure was unbearable for Hannah as women all around her were proclaimed "blessed mothers and wives." Hannah felt cursed and rejected by God.

Hannah was a **Victim** of criticism. She allowed herself to feel shamed and unworthy because others believed it.

She became her own **Villain** by accepting this faulty thinking.

She was a **Volunteer** for a beaten self-image as she allowed this talk to completely dominate her thought patterns.

She stopped eating and became "miserable" (v. 6).

Perhaps you can relate to a similar situation in your life, either as a child or as an adult. Do you remember a time when you felt inferior, unworthy, and low in self-esteem because of the words of another person or persons? You might have done as Hannah did. She disconnected from what should have been a healthy relationship and turned inward emotionally.

"No one can make you feel inferior
without your consent."
—ELEANOR ROOSEVELT

Ask yourself, *How much of other's thoughts and words are active in me right now? How am I responding to them?*

_____

_____

_____

_____

_____

_____

_____

_____

_____

_____

Proverbs 23:7 says, "For as he thinks in his heart, so is he."

That verse is true for both negative and positive thoughts. No matter how deeply rooted and distorted the picture, change is always possible for an almighty God.

> Do not be conformed to this world, but be transformed by the renewing of your mind. (Romans 12:2)

You may have been fed unhealthy thought patterns as a child, but you can break the cycle for yourself and for your child. Renewing the mind from unhealthy thinking is part of God's healing in our lives.

If these types of thoughts and labels are filling your mind like a radio on scan, it is time to reset and change the channels! Remember that God created you in His image! He has a plan for you! No matter what humans have said to you, it can never override God's intentions or His thoughts of you.

> How precious also are Your thoughts to me, O God! How great is the sum of them! If I should count them, they would be more in number than the sand; When I awake, I am still with you. (Psalm 139:17–18)

What will you choose to focus on? Being created in the image of God or man's silly opinion? Hannah chose God and she was transformed.

What happened? Read 1 Samuel 1:10–19 to find Hannah's steps to transforming unhealthy thought patterns. They will work equally well for you.

1. **Seek godly counsel always.** She went to the house of God to pray. "Hannah was so sad that she cried and prayed to the Lord. . . . She was praying in her heart so her lips moved, but her voice was not heard" (vv. 10, 13).

2. **Believe that pleasing God is better than pleasing man.** "I will give him to the Lord all the days of his life" (v. 11). Be open to God's direction and answer.

3. **Leave your problem with God in prayer.** "[I have] poured my soul out before the LORD" (v. 15).

4. **Change your behavior.** "So the woman went her way and ate" (v. 18).

5. **Have a devotional time with God.** "Then they rose early in the morning and worshiped before the Lord" (v. 19).

Hannah became a **Victor** and was no longer sad. You can too! What you must see in these next verses is that Hannah did not adapt to the situation, she overcame it. Hannah did not decide to look the other way. No, Hannah was transformed, and the result was overflowing joy. Oh, and I almost forgot . . . after she gave birth to Samuel, Hannah was blessed with three more sons and two daughters. The Lord answered abundantly. He does that!

Look at her psalm of thanksgiving: "The Lord has filled my heart with joy; I feel very strong in the Lord. I can laugh at my enemies; I am glad because you have helped me!" (1 Samuel 2:1 NCV)

Fill in your own name:

The Lord has filled _____'s heart with joy;
I feel very strong in the Lord;
I can laugh at my enemies;
_____ is glad because God has helped me.

Believe that the Lord will fill you with believing the best about Him, His plans for you, and about your own potential and worth.

unhealthy thought patterns

- **Judging your self-image by what others believe.** In Hannah's day, a great deal of a woman's worth in society and even in her own eyes was established by her ability to conceive, and the birthing of sons was like a double-point score! She could do none of this, and she developed her entire self-image around what others said, how they lived, and what they believed. No doubt she learned this from childhood and now was letting it affect her into adulthood.

Can you relate to these feelings? Think for a moment about childhood phrases or beliefs you carry with you. For example, "You won't amount to anything. Don't trust people. You're ugly or lazy. Stop being silly all the time. You failed. You can't do anything right."

What about things that have been said to you recently? On the job, by your family, by acquaintances? Are you measuring your self-worth by the financial standards of others? Do you think of a single-mom family as less of a family?

> When you talk, do not say harmful things, but say what people need—words that will help others become stronger. Then what you say will do good to those who listen to you. (Ephesians 4:29 NCV)

- **Regarding everything as a personal attack or rejection.** Hannah's husband tried to reassure her of his love. He asked her if he couldn't mean more to her than having sons. But Hannah refused to believe that she could be loved for herself. Instead she thought that love was dependent on her ability to earn that love. She couldn't understand that

Peninnah's taunting was out of the jealousy she could not control. It had nothing to do with what she had done or not done.

How much stress do you take on because you believe you could have prevented certain behaviors in others? If pure love and a sinless life could keep anyone from making the wrong choices, then Jesus would have been able to stop you and me from sin. But people have free wills and they react to life in their own ways. What other people do is about them, not you.

- **Becoming overwhelmed over small problems.** When Elkanah took his family up to Shiloh to worship the Lord, it should have been a happy time. But when Peninnah started to tease Hannah, she had a complete meltdown. She went in to pray but was crying so hard that the priest thought she was drunk. Neither your body nor your emotions can function in this type of reactive, emotional state. She became angry and depressed because she could not give her husband a child, yet her husband repeatedly told her he loved her anyway. She magnified the issue into a life-controlling event.

Focus on living in the present and trusting God for a great future. Check out the facts and allow yourself to experience feelings related to the genuine truth. When all else failed, Hannah just gave up and cried. She stopped eating and moved into the "nothing matters anymore" phase. In other words, she gave up emotionally.

People who say, "It doesn't really matter," are really declaring that they don't matter. Identify emotions that are appropriate for a situation and then give yourself permission to actually feel them before they disappear.

THINK ABOUT IT

Of the faulty thought patterns defined, the one that I think fits me the most is _____, as it prompts me to act in the following manner:

_____

_____

_____

_____

_____

_____

In your devotional time this week, pray that God would reveal changes to you—not because you are bad or inferior but because we strive to always be better for the glory of God. *Lord, what goals can I set in my spiritual life, career, social life, physical well-being, and service to you?*

healthy relationships do exist

Put your name in the following verses:

_____ *shall know the truth, and the truth shall make [me] free.* (John 8:32)

For as _____ *thinks in [her] heart, so [she] is.* (Proverbs 23:7)

Demolish arguments and every pretension that sets itself up against the knowledge of God, and _____ *[will take] captive every thought to make it obedient to Christ.* (2 Corinthians 10:5 NIV)

_____ *will not conform any longer to the pattern of this world, but be transformed by the renewing of [my] mind.* (Romans 12:2 NIV)

God created us with a basic need for a vital, growing relationship with others. We know this from His pronouncement in Genesis: "It is not good that man (or woman) should be alone" (Genesis 2:18). But many of us have experienced pain in relationships that have caused us to withdraw emotionally. The result is a vast feeling of aloneness, even in the midst of a crowd. To compensate we replace God's plan for genuine relationships with self-reliance and a hardened heart. The good news is that Christ understands this need and He has a plan for us.

Healthy relationships are God's remedy to meet the basic emotional needs we discussed in previous lessons such as approval, attention, affection, comfort, security, and respect. This may be in the form of family, friendships, dating, or marriage relationships, but the key word is *healthy*. We have discussed family and past relationship healing over the last few sessions. Hopefully you have taken time to write your letters or entries in your journals in order to deal with the unhealthy aspects of relationships that have the potential to destroy you and impact your children negatively.

Let's look at what **HEALTHY FRIENDSHIPS** look like:

F   R   I   E   N   D

Faithful, not fair-weather—A true friend will stand by you when it's not convenient. He or she will continually believe the best about you and call you to a higher standard.

> Friends love through all kinds of weather, and families stick
> together in all kinds of trouble. (Proverbs 17:17 MSG)

Jesus showed this when he continued to love and believe in Peter, even though He knew Peter would betray Him. Perhaps you have been in a relationship that ended badly because one or more parties decided to run away from the hurt instead of heal it. Now that you are emotionally healthy, you are free to love friends and family as they are. This is not the same as allowing emotional abuse; it is simple, unconditional love.

Roles vary—There are various types of friendships and each one plays a different role in your life. Let's look once again at the example of Jesus: He had *intimate friends*—His disciples who walked with Him daily. They shared everyday struggles, fears, and triumphs. He had *close, personal relationships*—Mary, Martha, and Lazarus. They respected Him, and He enjoyed their company. These were two-way friendships; even though they did not see each other often, each knew they could depend on the other. With all three, Jesus shared specific conversation, common interests, opinions, and accountability. He also had many *acquaintances*—those He met in the crowds as He traveled throughout the regions. Some of these were closer to Him than others, but each would play a part in encouraging Jesus, loving Him, and caring about Him.

Impact us—We become like the people with whom we surround ourselves. You can learn a great deal about someone simply by the friends she has. Gossips run with gossips. Negative people travel with those who will support or at least listen to their negativism.

> Do not be deceived: "Evil company corrupts good habits." (1 Corinthians 15:33)

Just as you tell your children to select friendships wisely, you must do the same. Choose godly and growing friends who will influence you in positive ways. Loving people does not necessarily mean taking on their problems or enduring their abusive behavior.

Choose carefully who you will allow to have significant impact over your life and time. These are your intimate, close friends. Many, many others will be acquaintances—people you are less involved with emotionally but with whom you are friendly.

Essential—We all need friends. We are relational beings. We were not created to live in isolation or to do life alone. There is no substitute for a friend who cares, who will listen, comfort, and reprove if necessary. Remember God's word:

> It is not good that man (or woman) should be alone. (Genesis 2:18)

Self-reliance should become God-reliance. This type of healthy attitude understands the need for healthy relationships.

Needs to be nurtured—Giving of oneself is a two-way street. If we want others to reach out to us, we must also make the effort to reach out to them. Jesus demonstrated this effort when He made the long trip to heal Lazarus, and when He met Peter on the shore to cook fish for him as a symbol of forgiveness and friendship.

> A man who has friends must himself be friendly. (Proverbs 18:24)

To make a friend, you must be a friend. Look for ways to give to others, and your aloneness will disappear.

Dare to hold yourself accountable—On one occasion, the disciples questioned whether He should be speaking to the Samaritan woman at the well. They were concerned about His reputation, and possibly, about Him being tempted. He gave them a sound explanation and set about to show her the way to eternal life. But many a "spiritual" relationship has had to be called into question for counterfeit circumstances. An *accountability partner* is an absolute necessity for your life.

> Two are better than one, Because they have a good reward for their labor. For if they fall, one will lift up his companion. But woe to him who is alone when he falls, For he has no one to help him up. (Ecclesiastes 4:9–10)

Begin today to ask God for a strong partner who will hold you accountable to your goals and values.

healthy dating relationships

Once you have learned to enjoy healthy relationships, you will not feel overwhelmingly alone. That isolated feeling drives many women to the wrong type of man. She finds herself making the same mistakes over and over again out of loneliness.

Anthusa was an intelligent woman living in the city of Antioch in the fourth century AD. She was married to Secundus, an illustrious officer in the Imperial Army of Syria. While her son, John, was an infant, her husband died, leaving her widowed when she was about twenty years old. It was a difficult time to be a single mother. Society looked down on such a life; there was little if any work for single mothers and no social services. What was a woman to do? Anthusa, history tells us, was a very beautiful woman. Many men came to call, hoping to court her, but she decided not to marry again, feeling that her child must come before her own happiness. She devoted her life to her son, and it was her goal to nurture in him the highest quality of Christian character. In his early years, she taught him to love the Bible and encouraged him to study and learn it. She instilled in him an intimate knowledge of the Scriptures.

John went on to become one of the great Christian leaders of his time, earning the name *Chrysostom*, meaning "golden-mouthed." Though he reveled in his classical education, the things of the Spirit he learned at his mother's home were what he credited for giving him the foundation he needed to succeed as a minister of the gospel and to become the man that he was.

No one is suggesting you be single forever. But, ask yourself: *Is dating right now a good thing for me and for my children? How important is dating to me? Why is it so important? How will it affect my children?* The last thing your child needs is one more painful relationship to deal with.

There is no doubt that being a single mom can be a lonely journey, but it can also be a very fulfilling, joyful one. Until you find peace in your life and enjoy healthy relationships, you will not be ready to add dating to your life. If and when you move forward into dating, you need to be ready to evaluate prospective dates just as you do prospective friendships.

Is there such a thing as healthy dating? Sure there is! How do we move from "friend" to "date"? Friend must always come first, and a careful checkup as the friendship develops will allow you to make the decision to move from friendship to courtship.

The first rule of dating: *Never date anyone you wouldn't marry.*
This eliminates:
- many wrong decisions and choices;
- temptations that should never occur;
- "Oh, how I wish I would have listened to others or to my own instincts!"

Now that you understand your own intimacy needs, you can begin to search beyond superficial characteristics in a dating partner. You need to identify the ability of the person to relate to others intimately on spiritual, emotional, and physical levels. Examining yourself in the light of God's Word is essential when considering choices about potential dating or marriage partners.

A friend is a candidate for a date when he exhibits characteristics such as:

D   A   T   E

Dependable—He is a *Protector*. He has a clear *Life Purpose*. He has a growing, vibrant spiritual life. He is patient with you and respects your values.

Questions to ask yourself:
- Is he loyal even when it's not convenient?
- Is he putting more/less into the relationship than I am?
- Does he try to change me into what he wants or needs (personality, sexual advances)?
- Does he support me emotionally or does he discount my feelings?

Accountable to others—He has good friends. He accepts responsibilities (beware of the "not my fault" syndrome). He is financially secure: saves money, lives on a budget, and doesn't need the immediate gratification of "things" that results in high credit debt.

Questions to ask yourself:
- How important are his material possessions to him?
- How does he treat his family? His possessions?
- Who are his best friends, and what type of lifestyle do they have?
- What kind of job record does he have?

Truthful—He is a man of integrity in business. He is moral in his choices, and he is scriptural in his decisions. He acts without sexual manipulation and does not dwell in fixing blame.

Questions to ask yourself:
- Are his values consistent with Scripture and with mine?
- Have I seen evidence of his character and his commitment to Christ?
- Have I ever caught him in a lie, even a white lie?
- Does he justify certain behavior or attitudes for the situation?

Emotionally healthy—He has a good relationship with his family. One thing to keep in mind: you will never be treated any better than he treats his own mother.

Questions to ask yourself:
- Does he love children and does he respect women? If there is even the suspicion of an issue there, run!
- What about prior relationships? Is it the "all her fault" conversation? Does he verbally run down the ex-wife or girlfriend?
- Ask about his childhood friends and previous experiences. Is there anything he has not dealt with?
- Can he initiate and receive emotional intimacy, or does he use sex as an intimacy tool?
- Is he able to communicate clearly to you and to understand your emotional needs, or to begin by trying to understand those needs?
- Is he loving and compassionate toward people?
- What do your trusted friends or family members think?

Dr. David Ferguson of Great Commandment Ministries gives this compelling argument in *The Purpose for Marriage*:

Achieving a sense of wholeness is not God's intended purpose for marriage. If that was your goal, it may have been born from unmet needs in childhood. When infatuation with a dating partner has a tie to your self-esteem, beware! You may be expecting union with that person to complete you in a way that only Christ can. Marriage was not intended to make us whole, but rather, in marriage, we are instructed to function as a whole. That has to do with how we work toward harmony and unity in all dimensions of our being.

Marriage is not the only path to a meaningful and fulfilling life. But that myth contributes to an unhealthy preoccupation with mate seeking, rather than a healthy desire that many singles will share. Pursuit of the Great Commandment leads to purpose for living that transcends our circumstances without denying them. God has called every believer to a life that contributes to His master plan for humankind. For many, that plan will include marriage, but you can rest in the knowledge that the timing and details of that part of your journey will be in His hands.

A HEALTHY RELATIONSHIP WITH GOD is the foundation for all others. Think for a moment about how deeply and intensely He loves you! It is almost more than one can understand.

As you read the following verse, how do you feel about God loving you so much? Before we can have a relationship with Christ, we must receive His gift of eternal life.

But as many as received Him, to them He gave the right to become the children of God, to those who believe in His

name: who were born, not of blood, nor of the will of the
flesh, nor of the will of man, but of God. (John 1:12–13)

The first step is to receive Him into your heart in the simple, humble act of salvation. *Lord, today I give you my life. Please forgive my sins. Come into my heart and save me. I receive the gift of eternal life that you died on the cross to present to me.*

Intimacy with God requires that we spend time with Him in prayer, that is, personal conversation with God. It is the only means by which a Christian can communicate with the Lord to ask for and receive help from Him.

One powerful, but simple way to have an intimate prayer time is to personalize Scripture as you pray.

For example:

I can do all things through Christ who strengthens me.
(Philippians 4:13)

Personalized: *I thank you, Lord, that I, ____(your name)____ can do anything through you because You give me to strength to do it.*

I will praise the Lord at all times; his praise is always on my lips. (Psalm 34:1 NCV)

Personalized: *Lord, I, ____(your name)____ am praising you for all that has happened this day, the good and bad, that I may learn and grow from it. Help me to think of good thoughts of praise throughout my day.*

If God is for us; who can be against us? (Romans 8:31)

Personalized: *Lord, help me to be courageous today, knowing that you are on my side and that is most important over anything else. I know You want good things for me, and no one can destroy your plans for my life.*

You can have confidence in knowing that God is indeed listening to you, even if it seems sometimes like no one else, including your children, will!

Then you will call upon Me and go and pray to Me, and I will listen to you. (Jeremiah 29:12)

THINK ABOUT IT

In which of these areas do your friendships seem the most lacking? Refer back to the F R I E N D acronym.

_____

_____

_____

_____

_____

Why do you think that is?

_____

_____

_____

_____

_____

What could you do, specifically, to encourage growth in one of these areas?

_____

_____

_____

_____

_____

Mom & Mentor Time

One of the ways that struggles in my adult relationships have paralleled those of my growing up years is: (For example: running away from problems, low self-image, fear of betrayal or abandonment, unresolved anger, etc.)

_____

_____

_____

_____

_____

Take some time to work on your relationships. Are they healthy? Think through each of these three areas and try to identify some strength areas and some growth areas for each set of relationships.

healthy relationships do exist

Your friendships:

_____

_____

_____

_____

_____

_____

Dating relationships:

_____

_____

_____

_____

_____

_____

Your relationship with God:

_____

_____

_____

_____

_____

_____

ten
turning stress into strength

Hear me when I call, O God of my righteousness!
You have relieved me in my distress;
Have mercy on me, and hear my prayer.
How long, O you sons of men,
Will you turn my glory to shame?
How long will you love worthlessness
And seek falsehood? Selah
But know that the LORD has set apart for
Himself him who is godly;
The LORD will hear when I call to Him.
Be angry, and do not sin.
Meditate within your heart on your bed, and be still. Selah
Offer the sacrifices of righteousness,
And put your trust in the LORD. (Psalm 4:1–5)

In the first verse of the Psalm, David cries out, "You have relieved me in my distress!" This is a picture of David in a cave, trapped and surrounded in a small area by the enemy. He asks God to come in and give him some "breathing room." Can you relate?

Eustress is good stress, such as a job promotion, marriage, birth of child, holidays, excitement and motivation about good things.

Distress deals with work demands, financial challenges, car troubles, the death of a family member, excitement over bad, and the fight-or-flight syndrome. Too much distress causes burnout in the inner spirit.

Both can be wearing on the body; both are cumulative in nature.

definitions of stress

Engineering term: Defines stress cracks or strain on a bridge or building

Sociology term: A state of extreme difficulty, pressure, or strain:

Medical term: A mentally or emotionally disruptive or upsetting condition occurring in response to adverse external influences and capable of affecting physical health. It is usually characterized by increased heart rate, a rise in blood pressure, muscular tension, irritability, and depression.

Two questions arose from David's time of stress:

> How long, O you sons of men, Will you turn my glory to
>   shame?
> How long will you love worthlessness And seek falsehood?
>   Selah. (Psalm 4:2)

Question 1: How long will you turn my glory to shame?

Let's review: The same **love** that compelled Christ to go to the cross and to forgive His offenders is the same **love** available to you right now and every day. The same **power** that gave Christ victory over death as He rose from the dead is the same **power** that is available to you right now and every day.

David felt that his kingly glory was turned to shame on several occasions, but we know the Lord has felt this same sadness. How would we, just mere humans, turn the awesome glory of God into lowly shame?

When we use statements like, "I just can't help it; I don't know what I'm going to do; Has God forgotten me? This attitude takes the glory of God—His power, resurrection, and love for us—and makes it impotent in our lives.

We turn God's power in our lives from glory to shame when we:

- allow our morality to be dictated by the world or our emotional need instead of commitment to moral excellence through God's Word;
- worry and fret instead of believe in His power and love for us;
- settle for second best in our lives because excellence is "too hard";
- refuse to believe that He is able to do exceedingly, abundantly, above all we ask or think.

"How long," He asks, "will you continue doing this?"

Question 2: How long will you love worthlessness and seek falsehood?
No one would admit to loving worthlessness, yet we do focus and prioritize our lives around it. The result is distress because we allow what others say to influence:

- How we think
- How we see ourselves, our self-esteem
- How we raise our children
- What type of friends we choose
- How we make decisions
- Our definition of success

You face daily stresses, but also major stress from important events and people in your life. Much of your time may be spent meeting other people's expectations or priorities, and this can cause you to feel victimized, overwhelmed, and out of control. You spend your energy on putting out fires and the stress of the immediate so that you do not have the emotional capacity to plan long-term.

Learn to distinguish what appears urgent but is not, what appears important but is not. We value man's opinions over God's truth:

- About ourselves
- About moral values

> *"When you reach for the stars, you may*
> *not quite get them, but you won't come up*
> *with a handful of mud either."*
> —LEO BURNETT

If you allow unfinished emotional business to crowd your heart and mind you will have:

- Dreams you want to start but haven't
- Relationship issues you need to sort out, but don't

In verse 2 of Psalm 4, the Lord adds an important word, *Selah,* literally, "think about it."

David comes back into the conversation to declare that God "sets apart" for Himself those who are godly. Some versions say this phrase should be translated as "made wonderful." The Lord "made wonderful" for Himself him the woman who is godly and is "set apart" for God's use.

But know that the LORD has set apart for Himself him who is godly; The LORD will hear when I call to Him. (v. 3)

This wonderful woman can be described as follows:

She has a quiet center. To be set apart is to have a quiet center and a life of purpose. This woman is proactive in controlling her life; that is, she plans and organizes her tasks, her priorities, and her energy.

Reevaluate your time to see where the time is going and how you can add important, personal tasks such as hobbies, family time, organizing, and planning to your life. Set aside time for relaxing and enjoying friends and family. Honor these commitments to yourself by letting others know that you are not available during this time except for emergencies. You will become a peaceful woman, not one who is defined by stress or often overwhelmed emotionally.

> *"You will never find time for anything.*
> *If you want time, you must take it."*
> —CHARLES BUXTON

- THINK! Did my choices last week lead me to where I want to go in life?
- We shape our habits and our habits shape us. What am I shaping?
- Inspiration gets you started, habits take you across the finish line.

She prioritizes her life.

> *"A major part of successful living lies in the ability to*
> *put first things first. Indeed the reason most major*

113

goals are not achieved is that we spend
our time doing second things first."
—ROBERT J. MCKAIN

She thinks through overcoming difficulty rather than giving up.

She lives a value-oriented life, not a task-oriented life.

She understands that she must be healthy—physically, emotionally, spiritually, and mentally.

PHYSICAL:

She . . .

- Understands that she must be strong and healthy for her children's sake
- Eats healthy foods to give energy, and provides the same for her children
- Goes to bed at least 20 minutes earlier, improving sleep habits
- Exercises or walks for 20 minutes, 3 times a week (this can be a fun activity with friends on your lunch break, before work, or in the evenings)
- Takes the stairs instead of the elevator
- Joins a gym or exercise class

SOCIAL/EMOTIONAL:

She . . .

- Spends time with people who care about her
- Regularly schedules phone calls to supportive people in her life
- Buys herself an inexpensive treat once or twice a month
- Hosts a simple fellowship in her home once a year

- Interacts with people in a small-group setting (exercise class, bowling league, Bible study, etc.)
- Concentrates on listening to others at least once a week
- Gives and receives compliments

It is not good that man should be alone. (Genesis 2:18)

MENTAL:

She . . .

- Understands the importance of a quiet heart
- Turns off the radio and/or TV for at least one hour—in the car or at home
- Writes down daily schedule and tasks and delegates what others can help with
- Thinks through what the children can do (fix dinner, do dishes, pick up, fold laundry, etc.)
- Finds a neighbor or friend who can help with homework
- Researches a hobby that is not expensive and passes this peaceful habit on to her children (reading library books, doing puzzles, etc.)
- Spends time organizing her day and her goals
- Reads newspapers and magazine articles
- Searches the Internet for information on specific topics of interest
- Spends time with people she finds interesting

"Man's mind, once stretched by a new idea,
never regains its original dimension."
—OLIVER WENDELL HOLMES

SPIRITUAL:

She . . .

- Develops a daily time of Scripture reading and prayer
- Listens to inspirational music
- Develops the habit of writing in a journal—positive thoughts, words of gratitude, and her feelings
- Finds a wonderful church for her and her children

In verse 4 of Psalm 4, David moves on to address the issue of anger: "Be angry, and do not sin. Meditate within your heart on your bed, and be still. Selah." Anger is a natural human emotion and is nature's way of empowering us to ward off our perception of an attack or threat to our well-being. The problem is not anger; rather, it is the processing of anger. Mismanaged anger and rage is the major cause of conflict in our personal and professional relationships.

Ask yourself: *WHY am I angry?* More often than not, the situation at hand is not the cause of your anger; it was the final push that put you over the edge.

Notice the directive to "be angry." There is a good anger; it is called righteous anger. This causes us to set things right and to declare truth. On the other hand, unrighteous anger is bad anger. It is reactive and gives birth to more anger.

All of this relates back to **Respond vs. React.**

Reactive people make choices based on impulse. They are like a can of soda. If life shakes them up a bit, the pressure builds and they suddenly explode. Being proactive means taking responsibility for everything in your life. It also means that you are free to choose how you want to react to certain situations in life.

> *"People are just as happy as*
> *they make up their mind to be."*
> —ABRAHAM LINCOLN

If you live proactively, you will find that your moods become much more stable. That is why the Scripture says, "Meditate within your heart on your bed" (Psalm 4:4). Get quiet at the end of the day and process the anger, the day. Be still. This simple act will change your life and transform your emotions.

Again, the Lord directs us to *Selah*, that is, "think about it."

What naturally follows a peaceful heart is a life of faith and obedience to the Word of God and the Will of God. In verse 5 of Psalm 4, David instructs: "Offer the sacrifices of righteousness, And put your trust in the Lord."

The word *sacrifice* means "to be, to remain so." There it is again: be still, build peaceful habits. Much stress is caused by indecision—what to do, what not to do. Most decisions can be made by using the Scripture as a guideline. Never stress over a decision that is clearly defined. Choose the correct action. Do right no matter what. Ask to be forgiven; be proactive in resolving the conflict; trust that God will help you through the situation.

Make a habit of doing the right thing.

> *"It is never wrong to do right and never right to do wrong."*
> —DR. JACK GRAHAM

Also, ask yourself: *Is this choice in line with my moral values, my highest priorities? Is this choice one my children would want to emulate when they are adults? Does this choice take me on a path toward my future goals? What regrets might I have? What are the benefits to my family?*

To be rightly related to God must include obedience to the words of Christ:

> But I say to you, love your enemies, bless those who curse
> you, do good to those who hate you, and pray for those who
> spitefully use you and persecute you. (Matthew 5:44)

To put your trust in the Lord is to understand the root word. In Hebrew, *trust* means "to be confident and sure." Put your confidence in the Lord to live peacefully.

> But without faith it is impossible to please Him, for he who comes to God must believe that He is, and that He is a rewarder of those who diligently seek Him. (Hebrews 11:6)

Mom & Mentor Time

When you hear the word *stress*, what is the one thing that comes to mind in your life? Your children's homework, your finances, work, relationships?

How much of this stress do I create for myself with deadlines, taking on too much, and lack of organization?

_____

_____

_____

What practical steps can I take to alleviate the stress?

_____

_____

_____

You can be sure and confident in this: God wants the best for your life!

Right now, visualize and verbalize the godly woman you want to be then begin to work toward becoming her. Spend each day matching your attitudes, conversation, and actions to that vision. Present yourself well. This means dress like a lady, and speak and act like the godly woman you want to be. Allow the peace in your heart to permeate your conversation.

Go back and look at the mission statement you wrote in chapter 6. Now rewrite your mission statement on page 120.

For example, *I am a godly, peaceful woman of purpose. My first priority is my children, and I am a woman of prayer. I take time to build peaceful habits for my children and myself. I apply excellence and patience to every task. I am an excellent (artist, designer, writer, teacher, etc.). I am healthy physically, emotionally, mentally, and spiritually.*

> But the fruit of the Spirit is love, joy, peace, longsuffering,
> kindness, goodness, faithfulness, gentleness, self-control.
> Against such there is no law. (Galatians 5:22–23)

MY MISSION STATEMENT:

_____

_____

_____

_____

_____

_____

_____

Write one thing you could do right now that could take you closer to being the woman you desire to be. It could be something as simple as making a phone call, buying a book, talking to a new friend, making an appointment, going online for research, or enrolling in a class.

> The steps of a good man are ordered by the LORD, And He delights in his way. (Psalm 37:23)

Write down one small step.

_____

_____

_____

Eleanor Roosevelt, one of our most famous first ladies, said, "The future belongs to those who believe in the beauty of their dreams."

**Congratulations, you are on your way to
a peaceful, confident future for you and your children!**

NEW START FOR SINGLE MOMS *is affiliated with*
THE GREAT COMMANDMENT NETWORK

The **Great Commandment Network** is a team of denominational partners, churches, para-church ministries, and strategic ministry leaders who are committed to the development of ongoing Great Commandment ministries worldwide. Great Commandment ministries help us love God and our neighbors through deepening our intimacy with God and with others in marriage, family, church, and community relationships.

The Great Commandment Network is served by *Intimate Life Ministries,* which includes:

The Center for Relational Leadership—Their mission is to teach, train, and mentor both ministry and corporate leaders in Great Commandment principles, seeking to equip leaders with relational skills so they might lead as Jesus led. The CRL then challenges leaders to train their co-workers in these relevant, relational principles because great relational skills can, and will, impact customer/member satisfaction, morale, productivity, and, ultimately, an organization's measurable success.

The Center for Relational Training—Through a team of accredited community trainers, the CRT helps churches establish ongoing Great Commandment ministries. Experiential workshops are available in a variety of relational areas: Marriage, Parenting, Single-Adult Relationships, Leadership, Emotional Fitness, Caregiving, and Spiritual Formation. These workshops are designed to support churches in their efforts to launch ongoing relational ministries.

The Galatians 6:6 Retreat Ministry—This ministry offers a unique two-day retreat for ministers and their spouses for personal renewal and for reestablishing and affirming ministry and family priorities. Co-sponsoring partners provide all meals and retreat accommodations as a gift to ministry leaders.

Great Commandment Radio—Christian broadcasters, publishers, media, and other affiliates build cooperative relationships in order to see Great Commandment ministries multiplied.

Relationship Press—This team collaborates, supports, and joins together with churches, denominational partners, and professional associates to develop, print, and produce resources that facilitate ongoing Great Commandment ministry. Experiential, user-friendly curriculum materials allow individuals, churches, and entire denominations to deepen Great Commandment love.

The **Great Commandment Network** is also served by *The Center for Relational Care*:

The Center for Relational Care (CRC)—Their mission is to equip churches to minister effectively to hurting people. The CRC provides therapy and support to relationships in crisis through an accelerated process of growth and healing, including Relational Care Intensives for couples, families, and singles. The CRC also offers training for counselors and caregivers through More Than Counseling seminars. www.RelationalCare.org

For more information on how you, your church, ministry, denomination, or movement can become part of the Great Commandment Network and take advantage of the services and resources offered by Intimate Life Ministries, write or call:

INTIMATE LIFE MINISTRIES
P.O. Box 201808
Austin, TX 78720-1808
800-881-8008

Or visit our Web site:
www.GreatCommandment.net